Back to Basics™

YEARS 3 & 4

FRACTIONS AND DECIMALS

Do you need to know the basics of fractions and decimals? Let's learn about them together.

Parents and carers are encouraged to read the explanation and practice sections with their child.

Ann Baker

Illustrated by
Janice Bowles

About this book

Each unit in this book begins with a brief **explanation** of a concept or a strategy. You are encouraged to read this explanation with your child and, where appropriate, to use everyday materials and examples to give meaning to the concepts.

We practise is a worked example for you and your child to discuss together, paying particular attention to the thinking processes required to understand the concept or apply the strategy.

You practise gives your child the opportunity to practise the concept or strategy. It also indicates how well your child understands the new material and often includes problem-solving questions to ensure that your child has mastered the concept or strategy.

If further support is required, you and your child's teacher can devise a plan to ensure that all the basic concepts are fully understood and consolidated.

The **Tests** at the end of the book are provided to check that the concepts are fully understood. Test 1 can be done after units 1–10 are completed and Test 2 when the book is finished.

Meet 'BOB' – Back Of the Book

At the end of each unit, BOB reminds your child to go to the Answers section at the back of the book.

Mathematical Content

This book has been designed to cover the concepts of fractions and decimals that your child will encounter in **Year 3** and **Year 4**. The units provide a comprehensive coverage of the following Key Topics from the **Australian Curriculum: Mathematics**.

Australian Curriculum : Mathematics

YEAR 3

Model and represent unit fractions including $\frac{1}{2}$, $\frac{1}{4}$, $\frac{1}{3}$, $\frac{1}{5}$ and their multiples to a complete whole (ACMNA058)

YEAR 4

Investigate equivalent fractions used in contexts (ACMNA077)

Count by quarters, halves and thirds, including with mixed numerals.

Locate and represent fractions on a number line (ACMNA078)

© Australian Curriculum, Assessment and Reporting Authority 2010.

Contents & Checklist

WRITING and TALKING ABOUT FRACTIONS

This is how you write one half as a fraction:

$$\frac{1}{2}$$

The top number in a fraction is called the **numerator** and it tells you how many equal parts there are.

The bottom number is the **denominator** and it tells you how many parts the whole is divided into.

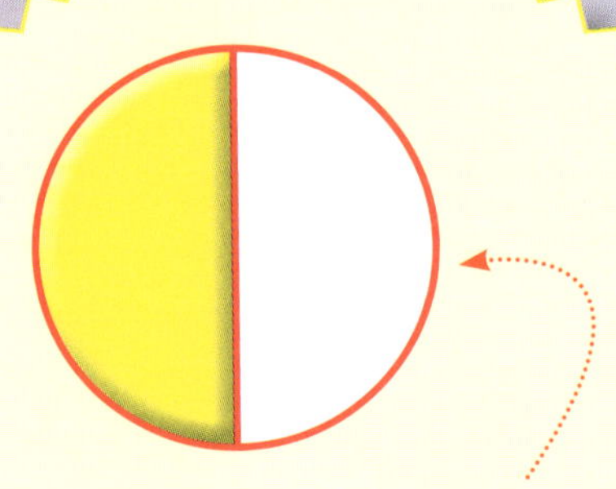

This circle is cut into **2** equal parts. Each part is a **half** ($\frac{1}{2}$) of the whole circle.

This is how you write three quarters as a fraction:

$$\frac{3}{4}$$

The **numerator** (top number) tells you that there are 3 parts.

The **denominator** (bottom number) tells you that the whole circle is divided into 4 parts.

This circle is divided into **4** equal parts. There are 3 shaded parts. Each shaded part is a **quarter** of the whole.

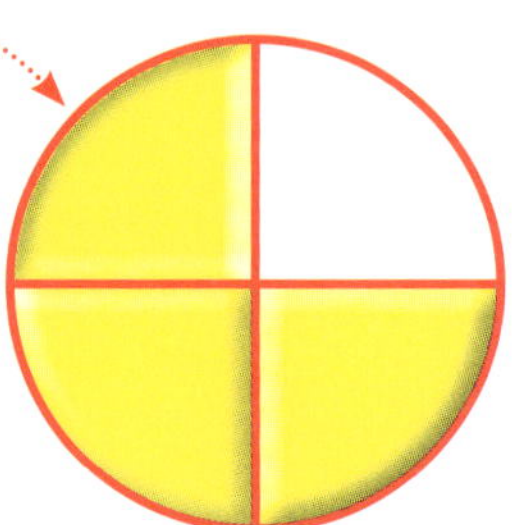

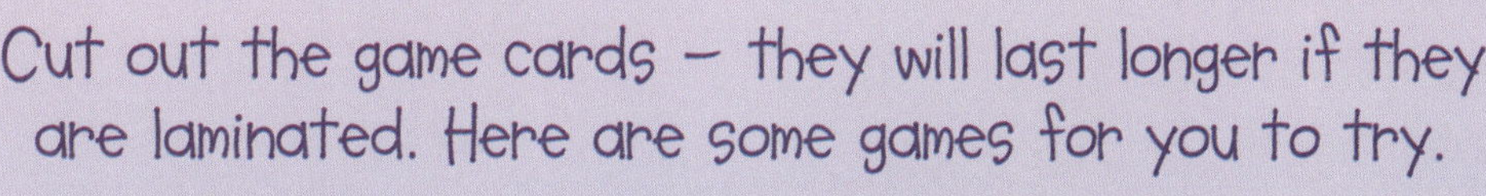

Cut out the game cards – they will last longer if they are laminated. Here are some games for you to try.

Fraction SNAP!

Shuffle the cards and share equally between two players. Each player takes a turn to put a card down. The first person to recognise and name an equivalent fraction adds all the cards on the pile to their hand.

The winner is the player who wins all the cards.

Fraction Fast Draw

Place the cards face down on the table. Both players pick up a card at the same moment and look at the fraction on the card.

The first player who shouts the fraction name correctly, wins and keeps their card (if the players shout the correct fraction at the same time, they both keep their card).

Once all the cards are used, the player with the most cards wins.

LARGEST FRACTION

Place the cards face down on the table. Both players take a card and the player with the largest fraction wins a point. Those two cards are then discarded.

When all the cards are used, the player with the highest score is the winner. In the case of a draw, both players win a point.

Players can use the fraction wall to check which fraction is larger. Change the game and play for smallest fraction, or fraction closest to a half.

Closest to $\frac{1}{2}$

Select only cards with related denominators, for example, $\frac{1}{2}$, $\frac{1}{4}$, $\frac{1}{8}$.

Place the cards face down on the table.

Both players then take two cards each and use the fraction wall or the number line to work out their value. The player who has the total closest to a $\frac{1}{2}$ wins a point. The cards are then discarded. Play continues until the cards are finished.

The player with the largest score wins the game. Change the total to 1, or use three cards to make totals closest to 1, $1\frac{1}{2}$ or 2.

NOTE: Games are meant to be fun and provide practice without stress. It is recommended that you stop playing while you are still having fun and then your child will want to play again another time.

UNIT 1 HALF, QUARTER and EIGHTH

When we share an object into equal parts, each part is called a **fraction**.

This cake has been cut into 2 equal parts. Each part is called a **half** $\frac{1}{2}$.

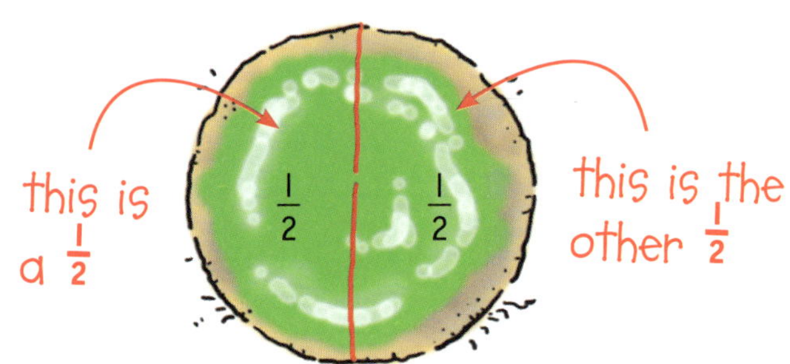

This cake has been cut into 4 equal parts. Each part is called a **quarter** $\frac{1}{4}$.

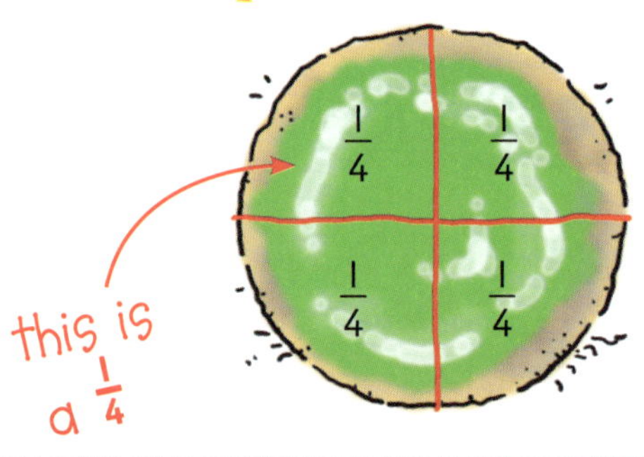

This cake has been cut into 8 equal pieces. Each piece is called an **eighth** $\frac{1}{8}$.

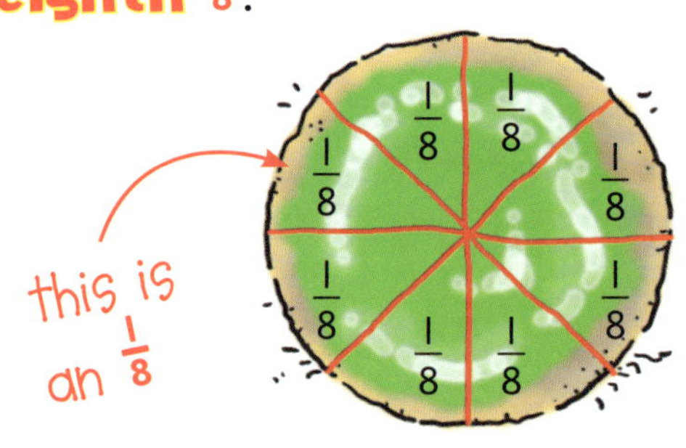

We practise

Cut this cake into quarters. Label each quarter.

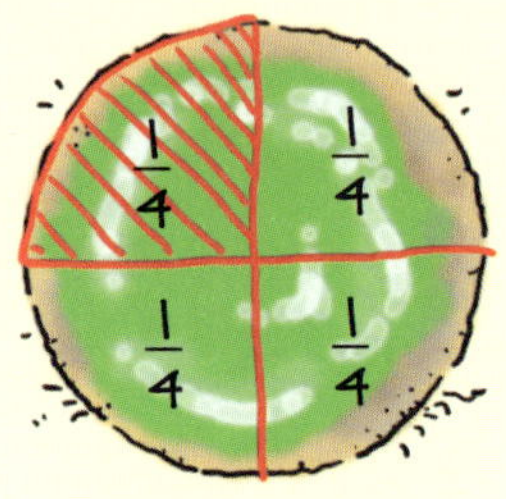

Shade $\frac{1}{4}$.

Cut this cake into 8 equal pieces. Label each eighth.

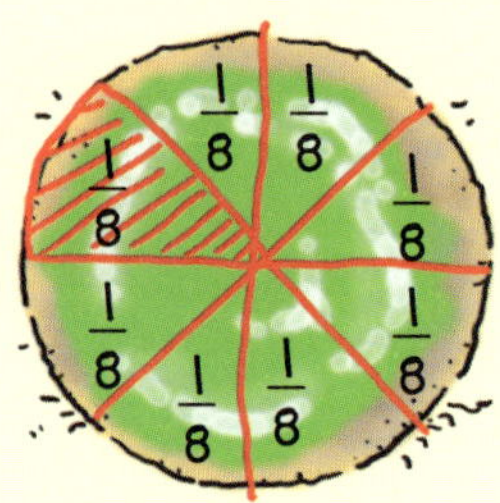

Shade $\frac{1}{8}$.

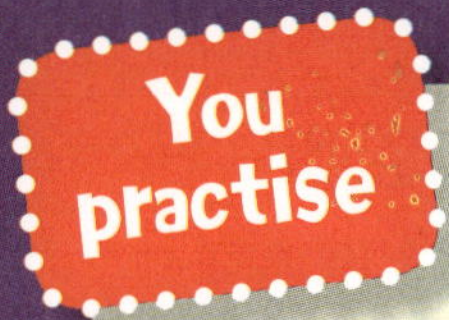

Show how to cut each shape into parts to make the fractions.

Cut into halves.

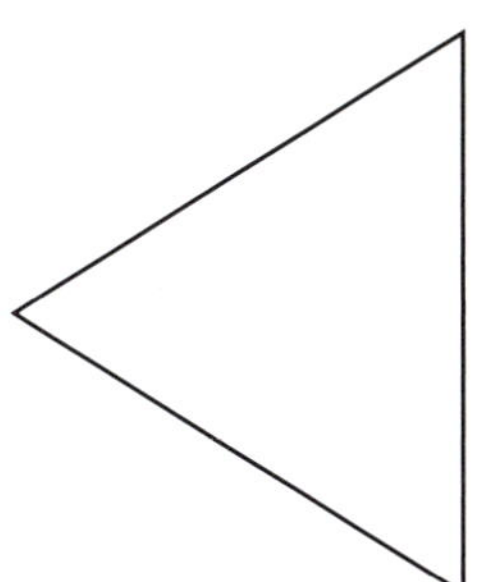

Cut into quarters.

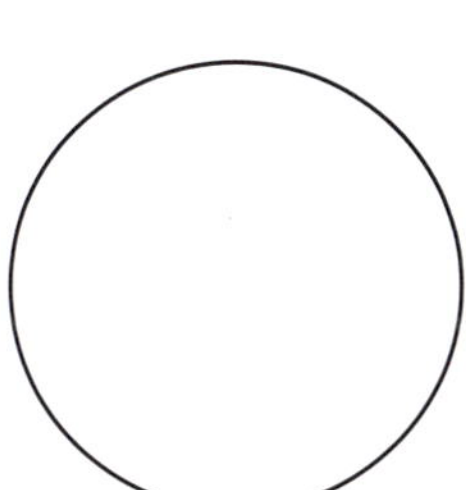

Cut into eighths.

Remember, all the parts must be the same size.

You practise

Draw lines to match the fraction names, fractions and shapes.

eighth $\frac{1}{4}$
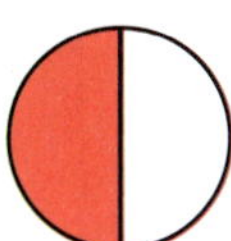

half $\frac{1}{8}$
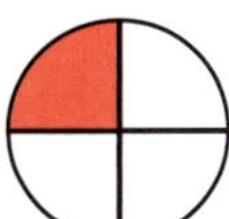

quarter $\frac{1}{2}$
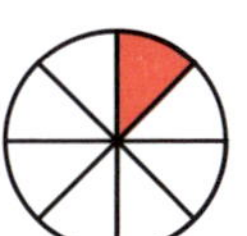

BOB time!

FRACTIONS OF SHAPES

What fraction of the pizza is this?

Knowing that **fractions** are **equal-sized** pieces of an object can help you work out what fraction of the whole pizza this slice is.

First, draw in the outside of the pizza like this.

Then continue the lines along each side of the slice, like this.

Now you can see four equal-sized slices. That means that the slice is a **quarter** ($\frac{1}{4}$).

Look at the steps for this slice.

Step 1

Step 2

Step 3

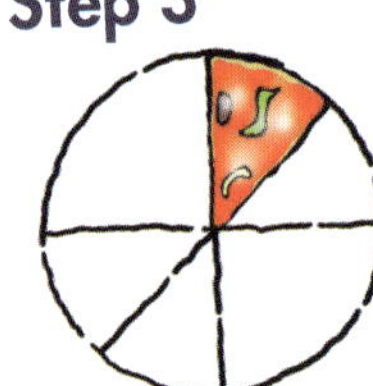

Step 4

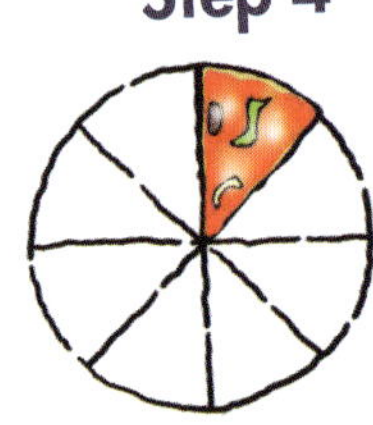

There are 8 equal-sized slices, so each slice is one out of eight, or an **eighth** ($\frac{1}{8}$).

We practise

What fraction of a triangle is this piece?

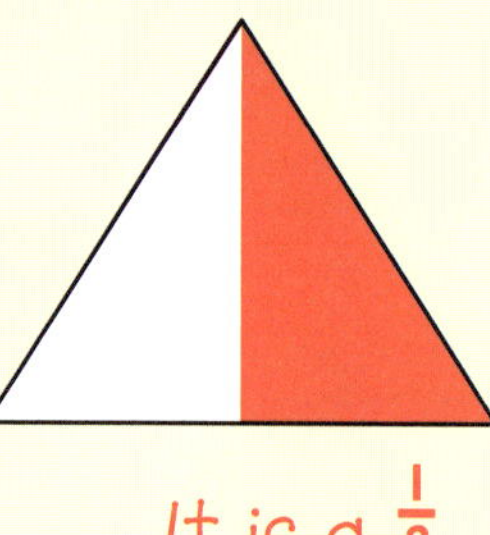

It is a $\frac{1}{2}$.

What fraction of the pizza is this slice?

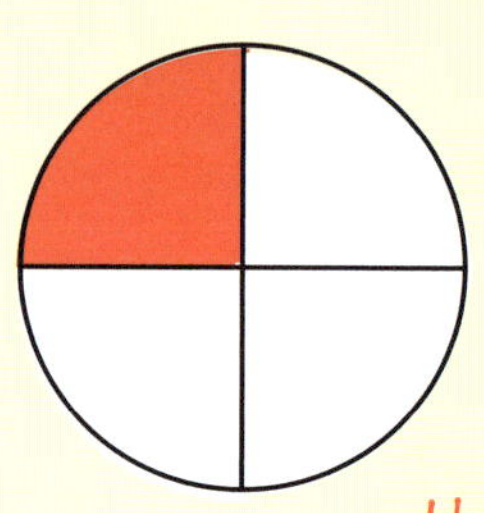

It is a $\frac{1}{4}$.

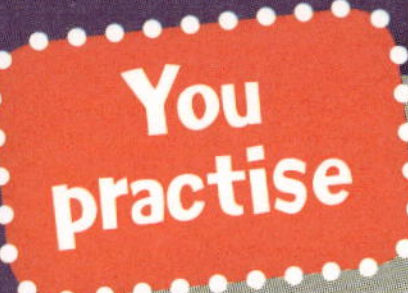

Match each fraction piece to the shape it was made from.

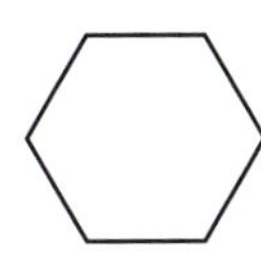

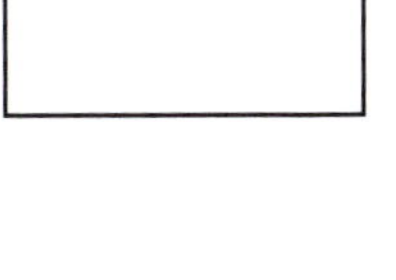

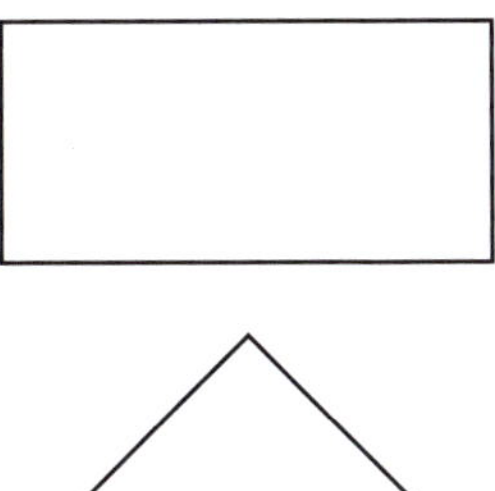

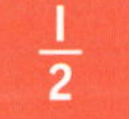

Remember to draw lines to check that the fraction pieces fit.

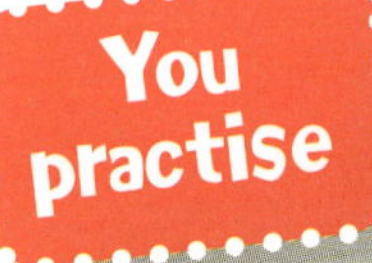

What fraction of each shape is shaded?

6

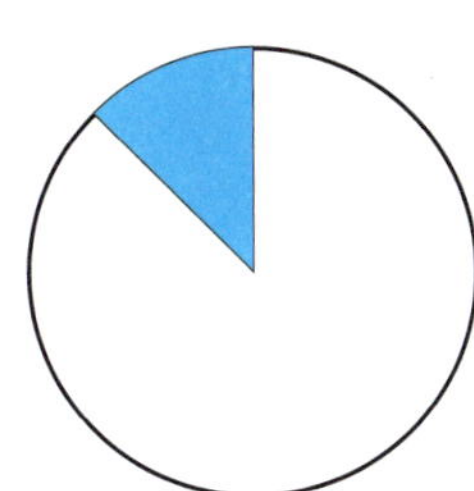

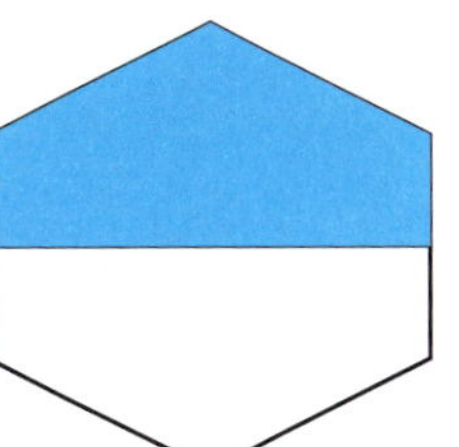

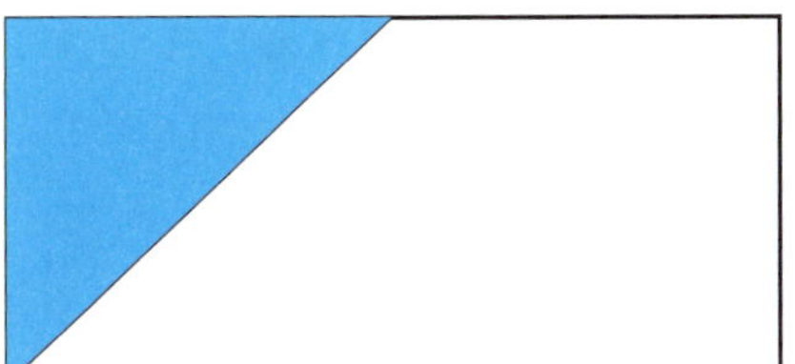

BOB time!

COUNTING FRACTIONS

Counting fractions is easy. Here are three **whole** rectangles.

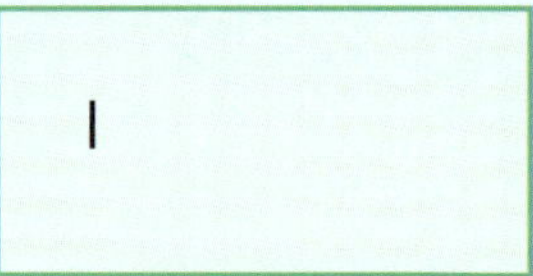

Now these rectangles have been folded into **halves**. Count the halves.

$\frac{1}{2}$ $\frac{2}{2}$ | $\frac{3}{2}$ $\frac{4}{2}$ | $\frac{5}{2}$ $\frac{6}{2}$

$\frac{6}{2}$ is how to write six halves using numbers.

Can you count in fractions?

You can fold them again to make **quarters**. Count the quarters.

$\frac{1}{4}$ $\frac{2}{4}$ $\frac{3}{4}$ $\frac{4}{4}$ | $\frac{5}{4}$ $\frac{6}{4}$ $\frac{7}{4}$ $\frac{8}{4}$ | $\frac{9}{4}$ $\frac{10}{4}$ $\frac{11}{4}$ $\frac{12}{4}$

$\frac{12}{4}$ is how to write twelve quarters using numbers.

You could fold them again to make eighths and then count the eighths too.

We practise

How many eighths are shaded?

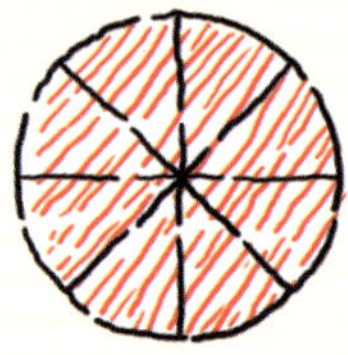
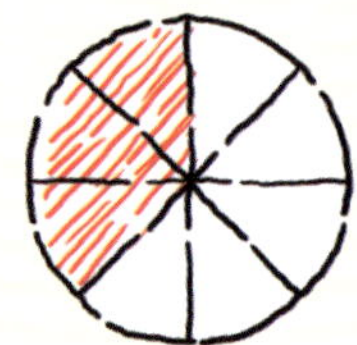

Count in eighths to find out.
Write the answer in words and as a fraction using numbers.

eleven eighths $\frac{11}{8}$

Shade fourteen eighths.

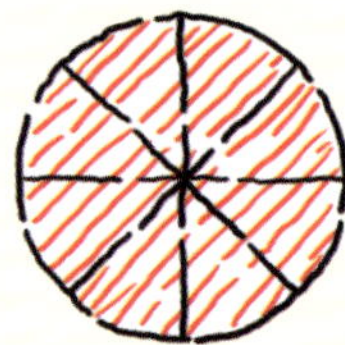
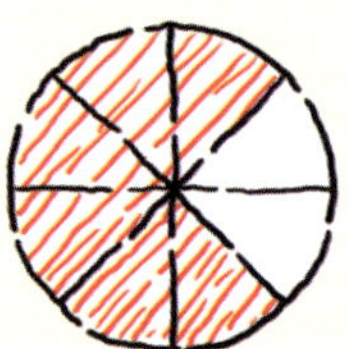

Write fourteen eighths as a fraction using numbers.

$\frac{14}{8}$

You practise

Count the shaded fractions and complete the sentences.

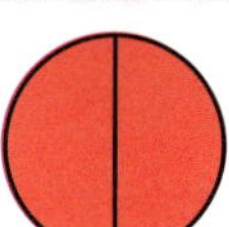 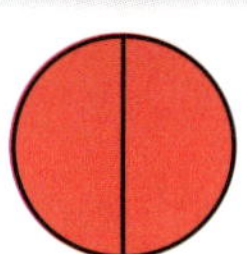 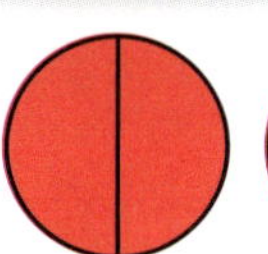 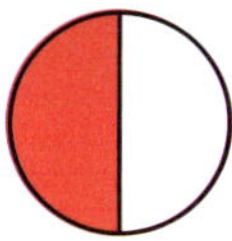

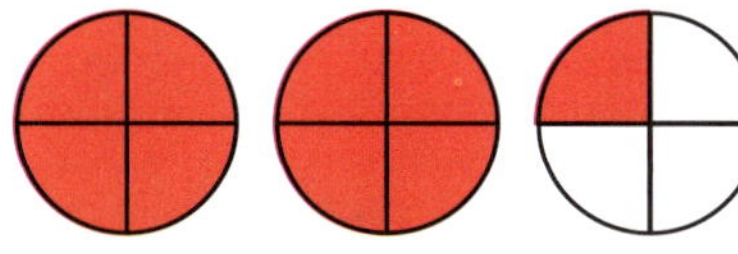
= ☐ ________

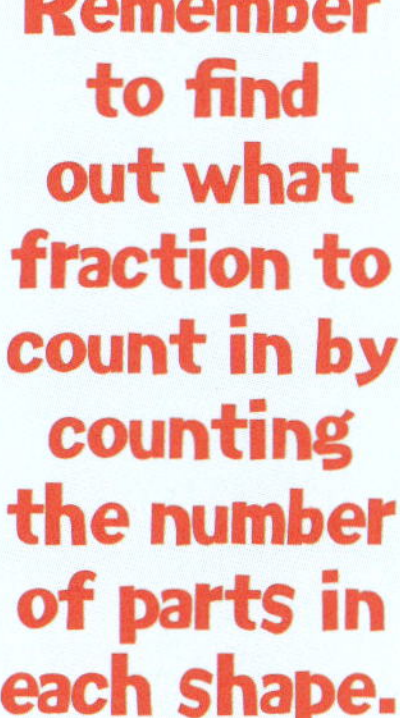

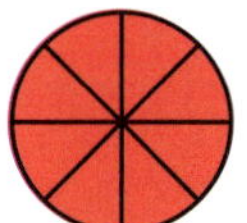 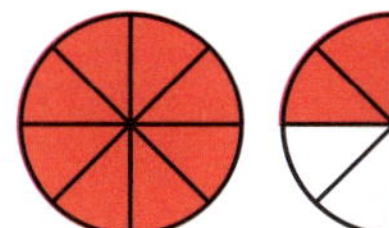

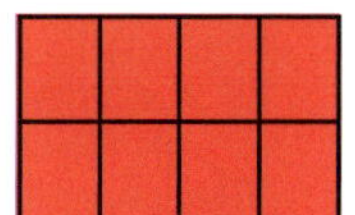 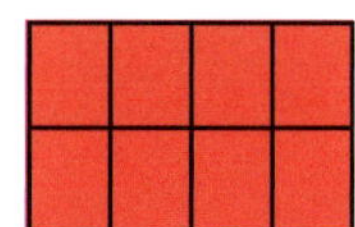 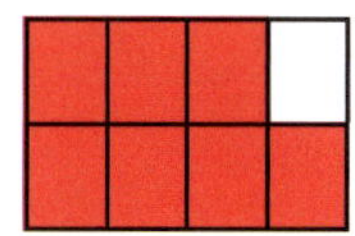

 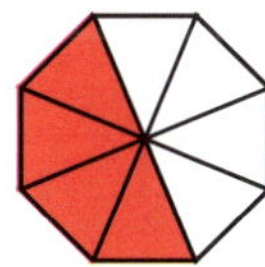 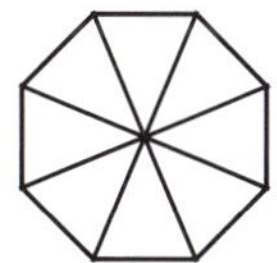

Count and shade each fraction.

$\frac{9}{2}$, nine halves
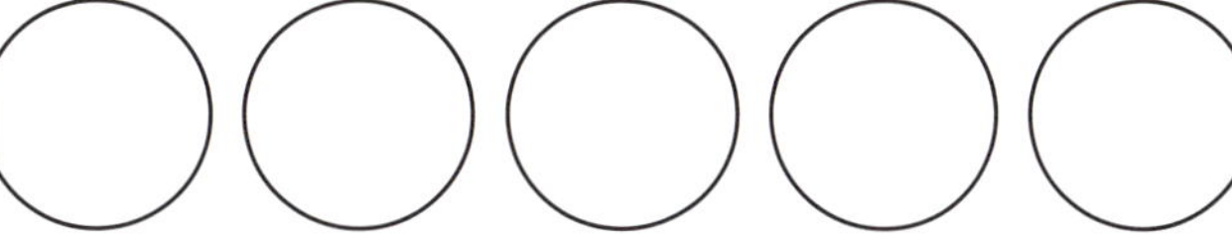

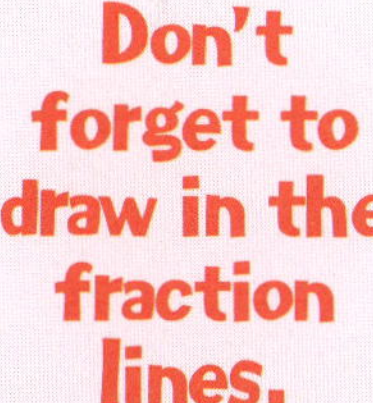

$\frac{9}{4}$, nine quarters

$\frac{10}{8}$, ten eighths
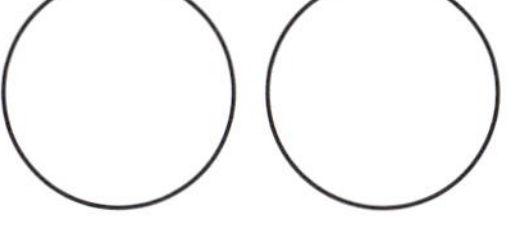

$\frac{15}{4}$, fifteen quarters
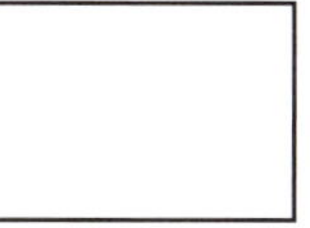   

$\frac{7}{8}$, seven eighths
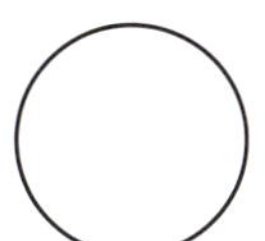

BOB time!

FRACTIONS OF COLLECTIONS

Here are 8 cakes on a plate.

If you share them equally between 2 plates, then there will be **half** ($\frac{1}{2}$) of the cakes on each plate.

If you share them equally between 4 plates, then there will be a **quarter** ($\frac{1}{4}$) of the cakes on each plate.

If you share them equally between 8 plates, then there will be an **eighth** ($\frac{1}{8}$) of the cakes on each plate.

Did you know that when you **share a collection into equal parts** you are also making fractions?

Share the cakes into 2 equal groups.

Each plate has half $\frac{1}{2}$) of the 10 cakes.

We practise

Share the cakes into 4 equal groups.

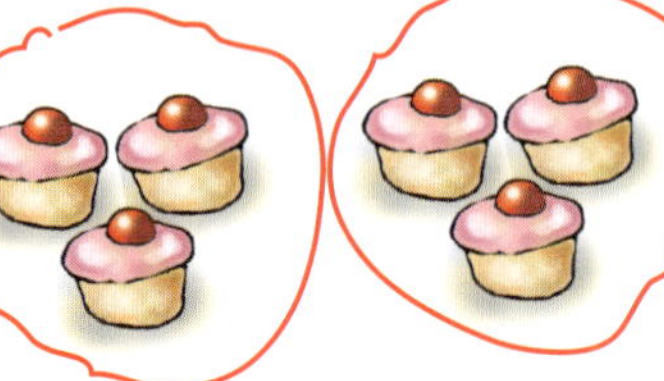

Each plate has a quarter ($\frac{1}{4}$) of the 12 cakes.

Show how to share each collection.

1 Share into quarters.

2 Share into eighths.

3 Share into halves.

4 Share into quarters.

Remember, make equal shares each time.

5 Share into eighths.

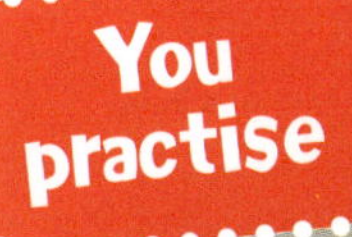

What fraction has each collection be divided into?
How many cakes are there altogether?

6    Each plate has ______ of the ______ cakes.

7 Each plate has ______ of the ______ cakes.

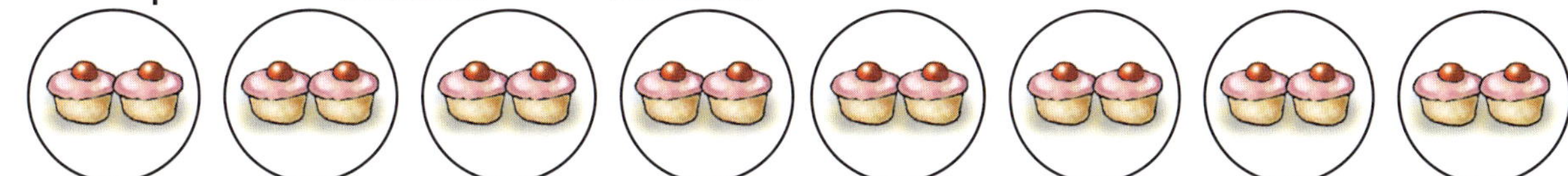

8 Each plate has ______ of the ______ cakes.

9   Each plate has ______ of the ______ cakes.

10 Each plate has ______ of the ______ cakes.

BOB time!

FRACTIONS ON A NUMBER LINE

Folding paper strips can help you to think about where to put fractions on a **number line**.

Take a strip of paper like this:

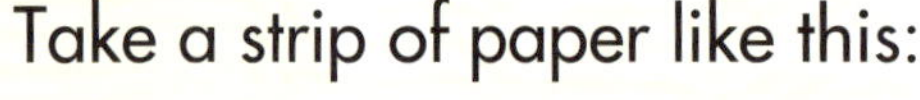

Then fold it in **half** like this:

Then fold it again into **quarters** like this:

Then fold it once more into **eighths** like this:

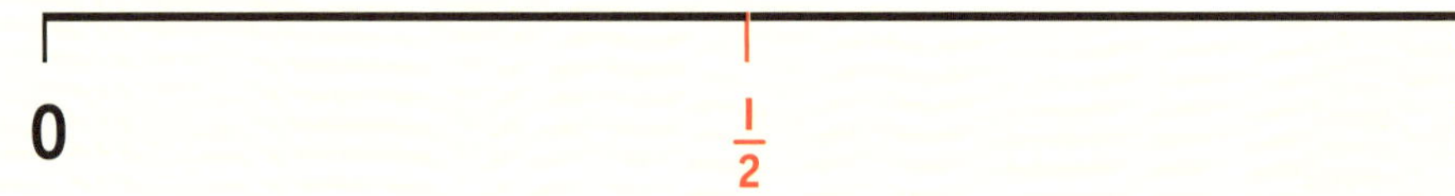

Half way between 0 and 1 is the halfway ($\frac{1}{2}$) mark.

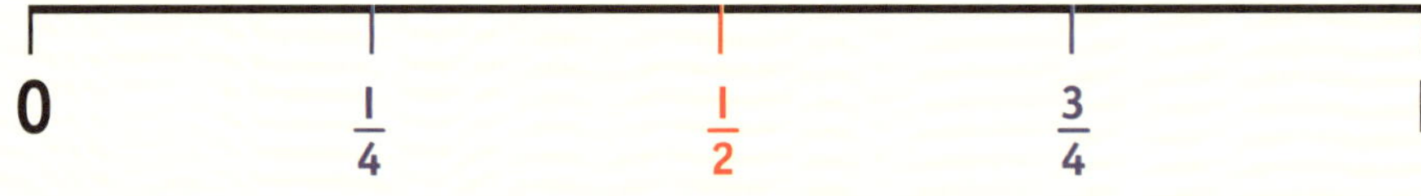

Then half way between 0 and $\frac{1}{2}$ is the first quarter ($\frac{1}{4}$) and then the other quarter can be marked easily.

0 — $\frac{1}{4}$ — $\frac{1}{2}$ — $\frac{3}{4}$ — 1

We practise

Where should $\frac{3}{4}$ be marked on this number line? Make marks to help you, but find $\frac{1}{2}$ first.

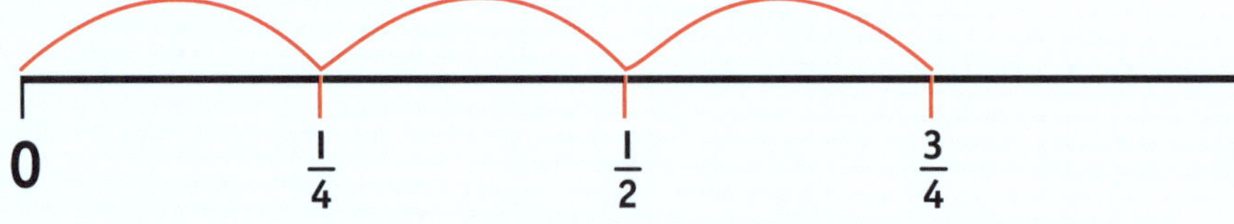

Where should $\frac{3}{8}$ be marked on this number line? Make marks to help you, but find $\frac{1}{2}$ first and then $\frac{1}{4}$.

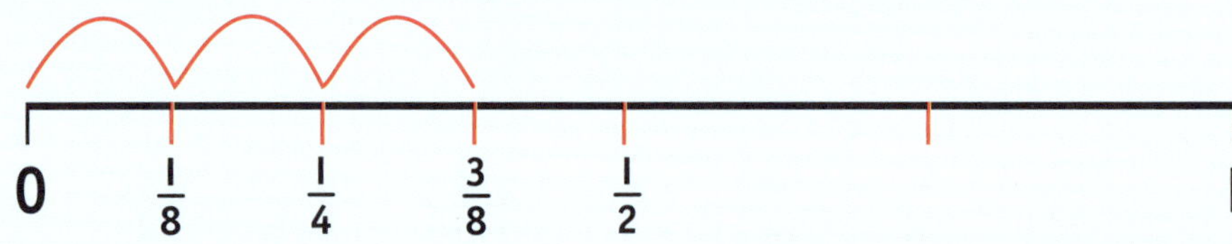

You practise

Mark each fraction on the number line.

1. $\frac{1}{2}$, half 0 ——— 1

2. $\frac{1}{8}$, one eighth 0 ——— 1

3. $\frac{3}{8}$, three eighths 0 ——— 1

4. $\frac{3}{4}$, three quarters 0 ——— 1

5. $\frac{5}{8}$, five eighths 0 ——— 1

You practise

What fraction is shown on each number line?

6. 0 ——— 1 the fraction is ☐

7. 0 ——— 1 the fraction is ☐

8. 0 ——— 1 the fraction is ☐

9. 0 ——— 1 the fraction is ☐

10. 0 ——— 1 the fraction is ☐

BOB time!

UNIT 6

COUNTING MIXED FRACTIONS

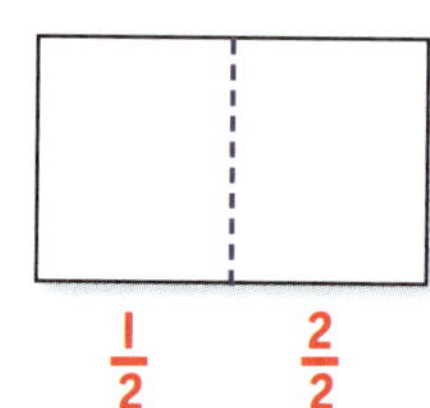

$\frac{2}{2}$ is the same as one whole, so you can count $\frac{1}{2}$, 1 and so on.

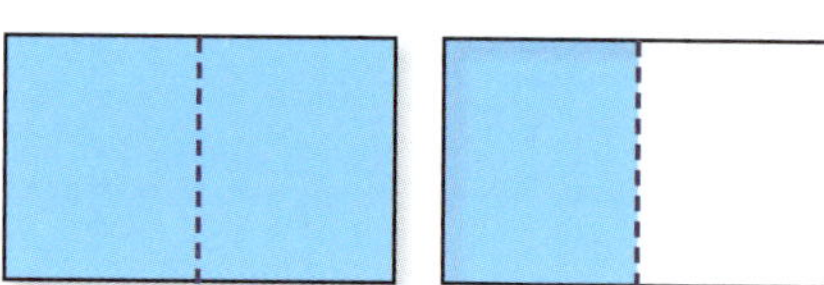

The shaded diagram shows one and one half, which is written like this: $1\frac{1}{2}$.

The big number shows how many whole ones there are. The fraction shows how many parts there are and what size the fraction is.
Fractions written like this are called **mixed fractions.**
In the diagram below you can count in mixed fractions.

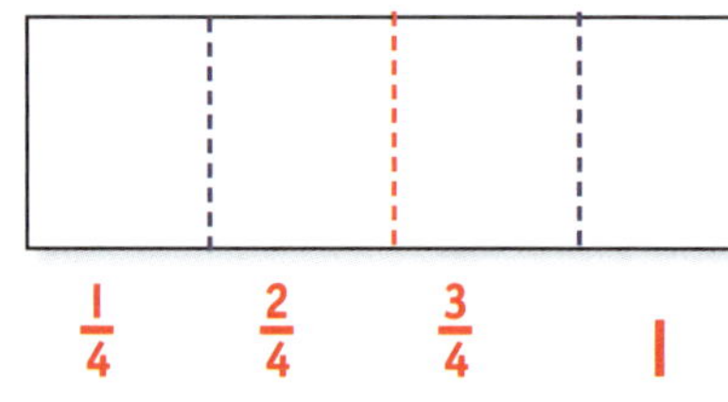

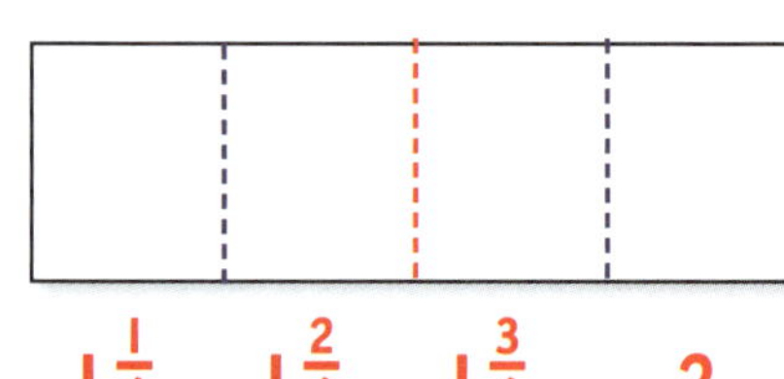

You can have fun counting fractions by including whole numbers as well as the fractional parts.

We practise

Count the shaded fraction.
What mixed fraction is shaded?

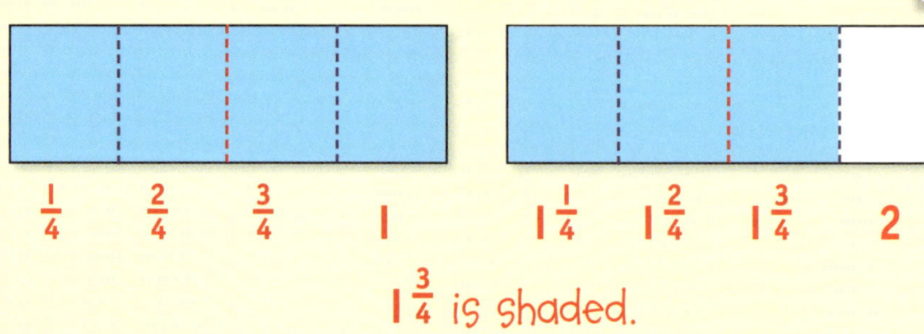

$1\frac{3}{4}$ is shaded.

We practise

Shade the shapes to match the mixed fraction $2\frac{1}{2}$.

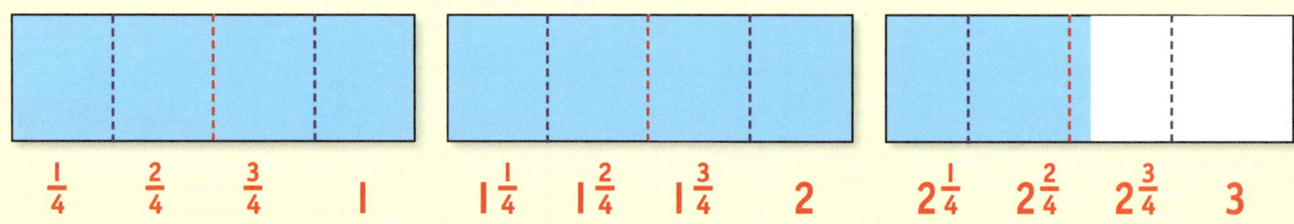

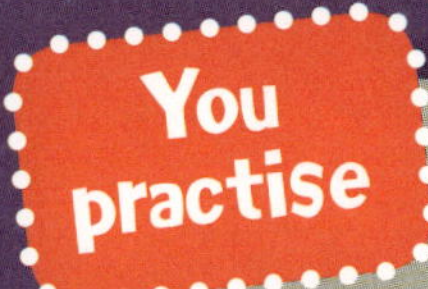

Count the shaded fraction.
What mixed fraction is shaded?

 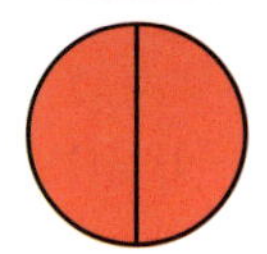 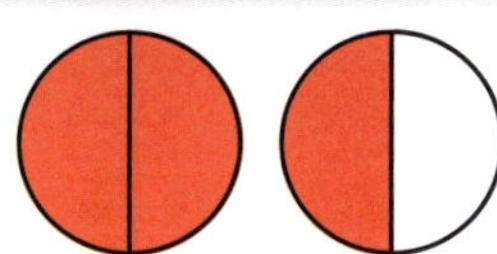  are shaded

 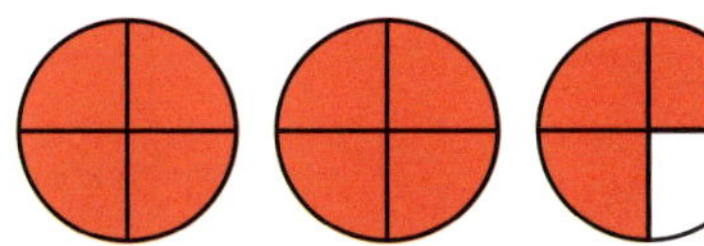 are shaded

 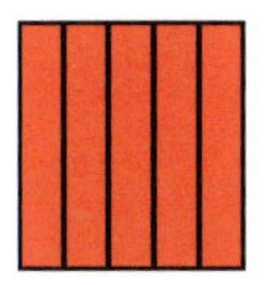 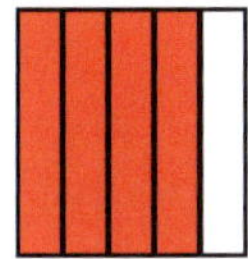 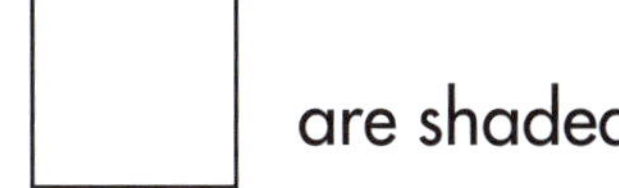 are shaded

   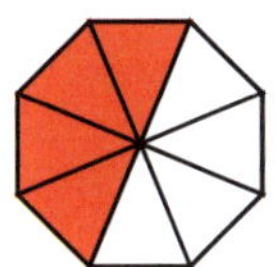 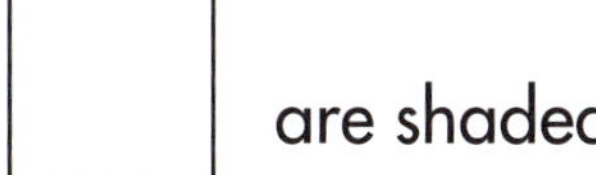 are shaded

  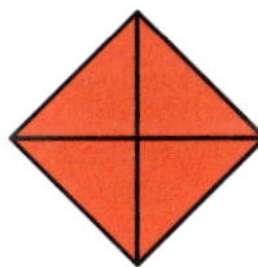 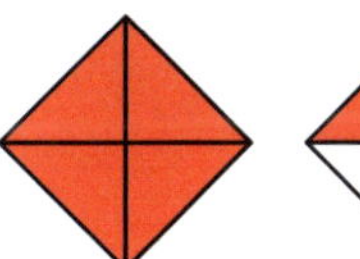 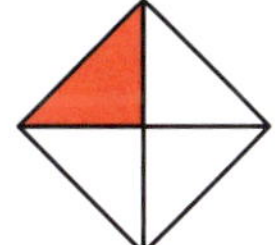  are shaded

You practise

Shade the shapes to match the mixed fractions.

 $2\frac{1}{2}$   

 $3\frac{1}{4}$    

 $1\frac{5}{8}$  

 $1\frac{3}{4}$  

 $2\frac{7}{8}$   

Remember to draw in the fractions first.

BOB time!

UNIT 7

COMPARING FRACTIONS

Which fraction is larger, $\frac{1}{2}$ or $\frac{1}{8}$?

A lot of people think that $\frac{1}{8}$ is larger than $\frac{1}{2}$ because 8 is a larger number than 2. But fractions do not work like that.

$\frac{1}{8}$ means that something has been made into 8 equal parts, whereas $\frac{1}{2}$ means that something has been cut into 2 equal parts. The halves would be much larger than the eighths.

Look at the two identical paper strips below; one strip has been folded into **halves** and the pieces are quite **large**.
The other strip has been folded into **eighths** and each piece is quite **small**.

You can compare the same fractions on a number line like this.
There are eight jumps here and each jump is quite small.

We practise

Use the number line to show which fraction is larger, $\frac{5}{8}$ or $\frac{1}{2}$.

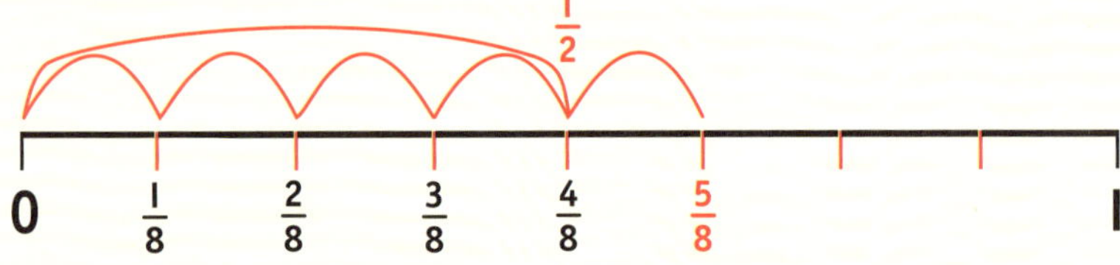

$\frac{5}{8}$ is larger than $\frac{1}{2}$

Mark the half, then the quarters and then the eighths.

Which fraction comes between 0 and $\frac{1}{4}$?
Use the number line to work it out.

$\frac{1}{8}$ comes between 0 and $\frac{1}{4}$

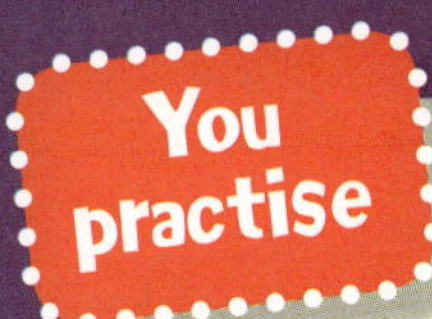

Which is the larger in these pairs of fractions?

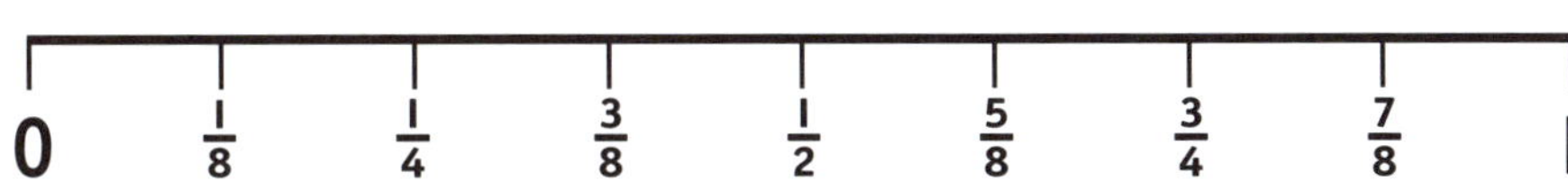

1. $\frac{5}{8}$ or $\frac{3}{4}$ ____ is larger than ____

2. $\frac{3}{4}$ or $\frac{7}{8}$ ____ is larger than ____

3. $\frac{1}{2}$ or $\frac{3}{8}$ ____ is larger than ____

4. $\frac{3}{8}$ or $\frac{3}{4}$ ____ is larger than ____

Use the number line to help you.

What is one fraction that comes between each of these pairs of fractions?

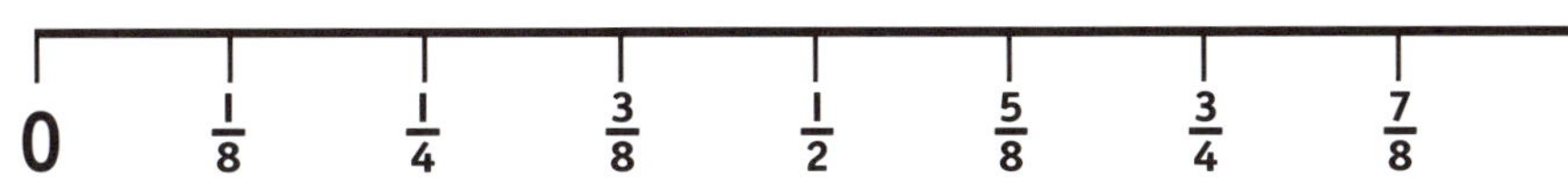

5. ____ is between $\frac{1}{2}$ and 1

6. ____ is between $\frac{1}{4}$ and $\frac{3}{4}$

7. ____ is between $\frac{1}{8}$ and $\frac{1}{2}$

8. ____ is between $\frac{1}{2}$ and $\frac{3}{4}$

BOB time!

EQUIVALENT FRACTIONS

If you fold a piece of paper in half and then in half again, you will see that $\frac{2}{4}$ **is the same as** $\frac{1}{2}$.

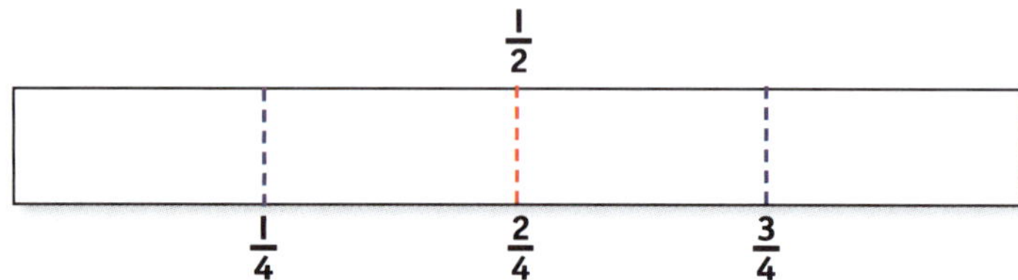

$\frac{2}{4}$ is **equivalent** to (same as) $\frac{1}{2}$.

Can you see a pattern in the sequence of equivalent fractions?

If you refold the paper and then fold it in half again, it makes eighths. If you open it up you can find more **equivalent fractions**.

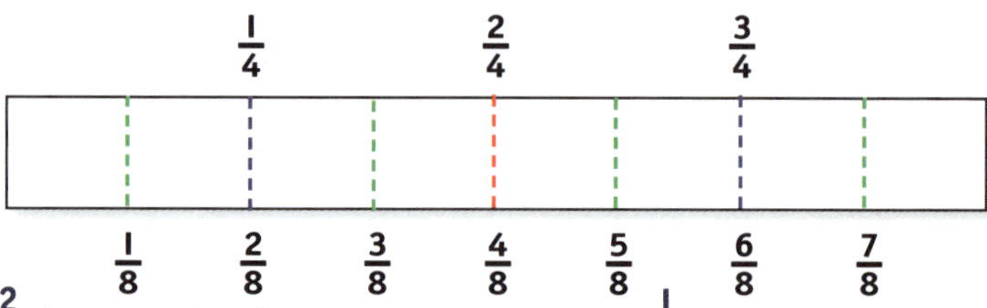

$\frac{2}{8}$ **is equivalent to** (same as) $\frac{1}{4}$.

$\frac{4}{8}$ **is equivalent to** (same as) $\frac{2}{4}$ or $\frac{1}{2}$.

$\frac{4}{8}$, $\frac{2}{4}$ and $\frac{1}{2}$ **are all equivalent to each other.**

We practise

Shade the diagram to show how many quarters are needed to fill half of the rectangle.

2 quarters are needed to fill $\frac{1}{2}$ of the rectangle.

Shade the diagram to show an equivalent fraction.

$\frac{6}{8}$ is equivalent to $\frac{3}{4}$.

You practise

Shade the diagram to show …

 How many quarters are equivalent to $\frac{1}{2}$

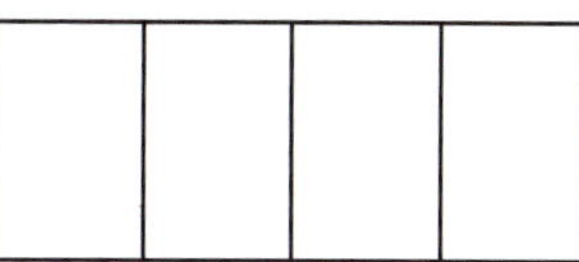

 How many eighths are equivalent to $\frac{1}{2}$

 How many eighths are equivalent to 1

 How many eighths are equivalent to $\frac{3}{4}$

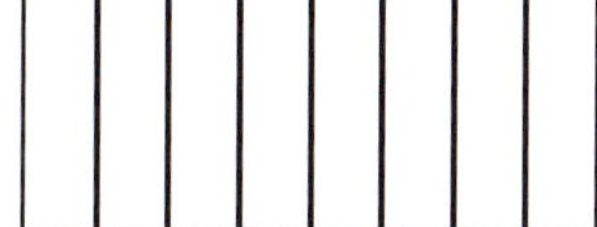

 How many eighths are equivalent to 2

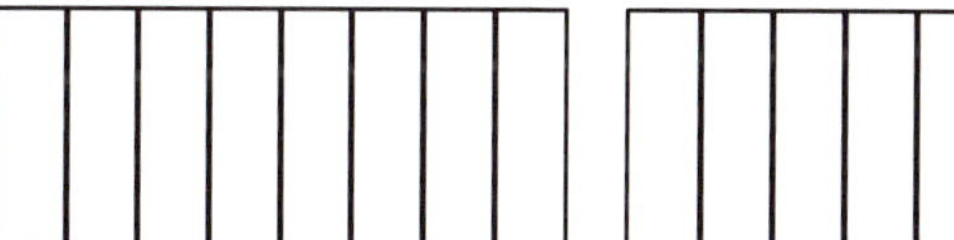

You practise

Complete the equivalent fraction sentences.

 $\frac{1}{2}$ is equivalent to ________ and ________

 $\frac{6}{8}$ is equivalent to ________

Remember, it helps to fold a piece of paper into eighths.

 $\frac{3}{4}$ is equivalent to ________

 $\frac{5}{4}$ is equivalent to ________

 $\frac{16}{8}$ is equivalent to ________ , ________ and ________

BOB time!

FRACTIONS EVERYWHERE

There are lots of places where fractions are used if you look carefully.

Here are three places in the kitchen where fractions are used.

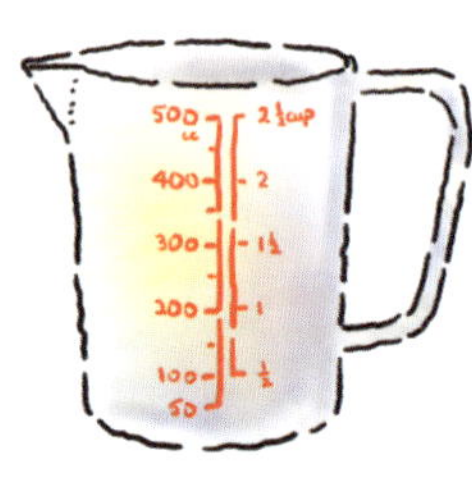

There are lots of fractions in recipes, such as $\frac{1}{2}$ cup of sugar.

If you only want to make half a recipe, then fractions are very useful.

If I don't have a half cup, but I have a quarter cup, I can use it twice to measure half a cup.

The recipe asks for $\frac{1}{2}$ cup of milk.
But I only want to make half the mix.
Mark the cup that I need to use.

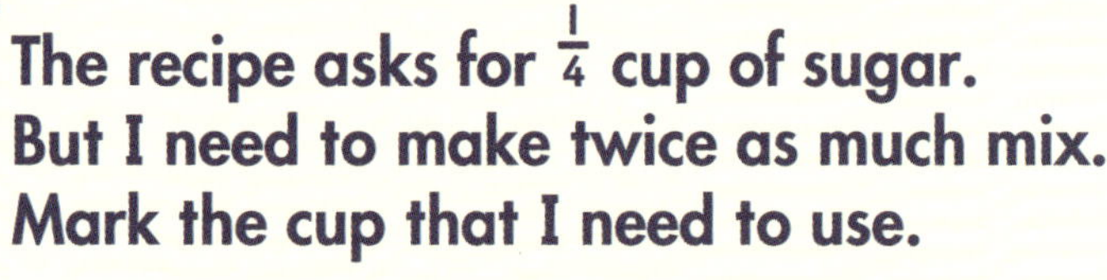

The recipe asks for $\frac{1}{4}$ cup of sugar.
But I need to make twice as much mix.
Mark the cup that I need to use.

Making chocolate chip cookies.

Recipe

2 cups of flour
1 cup of sugar
1 teaspoon of salt
$\frac{1}{4}$ cup of cocoa
2 eggs
80 chocolate chips
$\frac{1}{2}$ cup of milk

How much to make half as much mix as the recipe says?

____________ cup of flour
____________ cup of sugar
____________ teaspoon of salt
____________ cup of cocoa
____________ egg
____________ chocolate chips
____________ cup of milk

Recipe

2 cups of flour
1 cup of sugar
1 teaspoon of salt
$\frac{1}{4}$ cup of cocoa
2 eggs
80 chocolate chips
$\frac{1}{2}$ cup of milk

How much to make twice as much mix as the recipe says?

____________ cups of flour
____________ cups of sugar
____________ teaspoons of salt
____________ cup of cocoa
____________ eggs
____________ chocolate chips
____________ cup of milk

BOB time!

PROBLEM SOLVING WITH FRACTIONS

A fraction problem

Imagine that you have 3 different pizzas to share between 4 people – Max, Carlos, Jo and Kym. Everyone must have an equal share of each pizza. How should the pizzas be cut?

What fraction of the pizzas should each person receive?

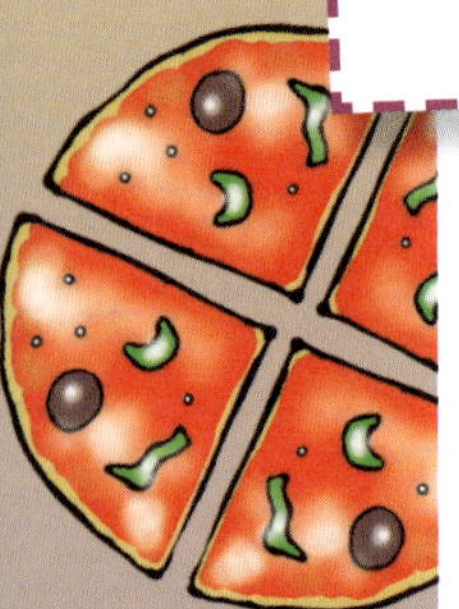

Notice how the important information is highlighted in blue.
Notice how what has to be found out is highlighted in pink.
This helps you to find all of the important information in this problem.
Drawing the pizzas then cutting them into fractions is a good starting point for this problem.

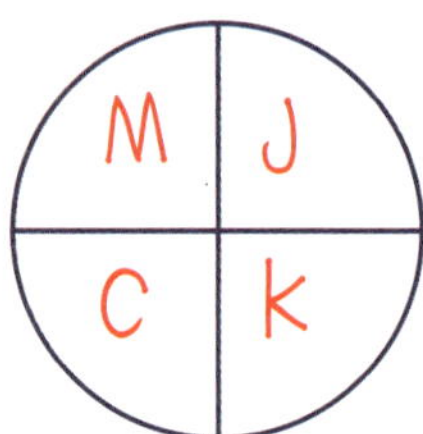

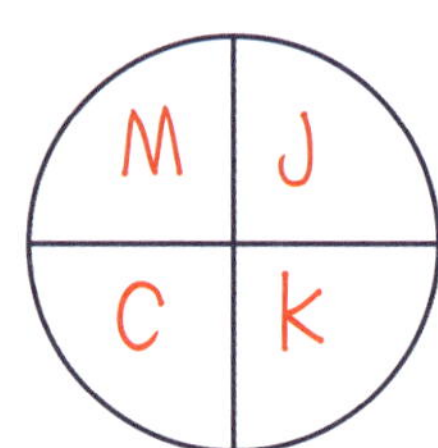

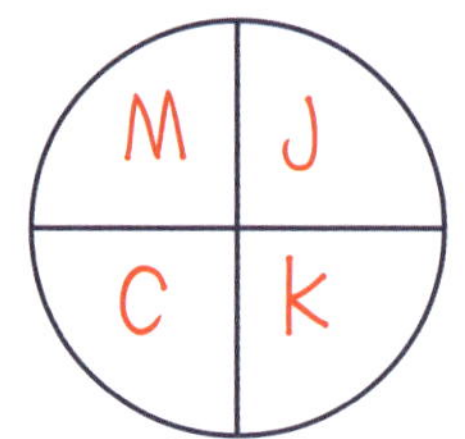

Max, Carlos, Jo and Kym get $\frac{3}{4}$ each.

Using initials helps make it clear.

Highlight the important information and what you have to find out in this problem.

A pizza was cut into eighths.
Carlos ate $\frac{3}{8}$ and Storm ate $\frac{1}{4}$.
How much pizza is left for Max?
Draw a picture to solve the problem.

We practise

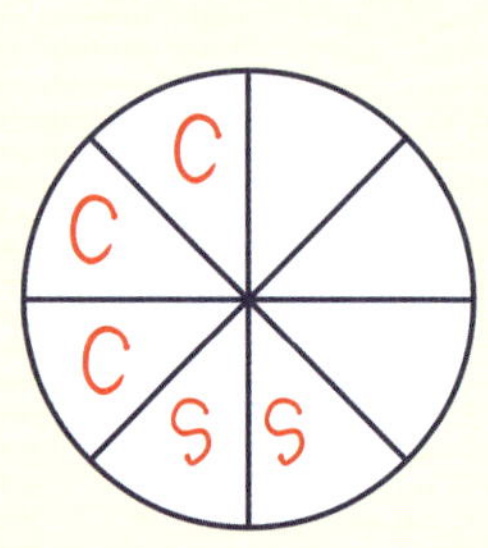

Max will have $\frac{3}{8}$ of the pizza.

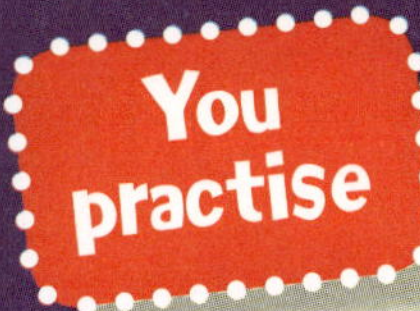

Highlight the important information and solve the problems.

1. Storm ate $\frac{1}{4}$ of a chocolate bar. How much is left? _____

2. Max is cross because only $\frac{1}{8}$ of the pizza is left for him.
How much had already been eaten?_____

Remember, drawing pictures helps.

3. Storm cut 5 apples into quarters.
How many quarters does this make?_____

4. Carlos shared a packet of 24 lollies into eighths.
He gave $\frac{3}{8}$ of them to his brother Max. How many lollies did Carlos give to Max?_____

5. Mike was given 6 marbles. This is $\frac{1}{4}$ of the marbles in the bag.
How many marbles are there altogether?_____

6. Storm took half of the bag of 16 marbles. Max and Carlos shared the rest. What fraction of the marbles do Max and Carlos each have?_____
How many marbles do Max and Carlos each have?_____

7. All of the pizza was eaten. Storm ate $\frac{1}{4}$, Max ate $\frac{1}{2}$, and then Storm ate the rest of the pizza.
How much pizza did Storm eat?_____

8. The recipe requires $1\frac{1}{2}$ cups of milk. How much milk would be required for half of the recipe?_____

9. The soccer team has won 12 matches this season. $\frac{1}{4}$ of the matches they won were played away from home.
How many matches were won at home?_____

10. Max had $10. He spent $\frac{1}{2}$ of it and then gave Storm $2.
How much money does Max have left?_____

BOB time!

UNIT 11 THIRD, SIXTH, FIFTH and TENTH

Remember, when you make thirds you only need to make two folds.

This rectangle has been folded into **3 equal parts**. Each part is called a **third** ($\frac{1}{3}$).

$\frac{1}{3}$	$\frac{1}{3}$	$\frac{1}{3}$

This rectangle has been folded into **thirds** and then folded in **half** through the middle to make **6 equal parts**. Each part is called a **sixth** ($\frac{1}{6}$).

$\frac{1}{6}$	$\frac{1}{6}$	$\frac{1}{6}$
$\frac{1}{6}$	$\frac{1}{6}$	$\frac{1}{6}$

Fifths ($\frac{1}{5}$) are a bit difficult to fold, so we measured a 5cm-long rectangle and then folded it at every centimetre to make **5 equal parts**.

$\frac{1}{5}$	$\frac{1}{5}$	$\frac{1}{5}$	$\frac{1}{5}$	$\frac{1}{5}$

It is easy to halve this rectangle again to make **10 equal parts**. Each part is called a **tenth** ($\frac{1}{10}$).

$\frac{1}{10}$	$\frac{1}{10}$	$\frac{1}{10}$	$\frac{1}{10}$	$\frac{1}{10}$
$\frac{1}{10}$	$\frac{1}{10}$	$\frac{1}{10}$	$\frac{1}{10}$	$\frac{1}{10}$

We practise

Has this shape been cut into thirds?

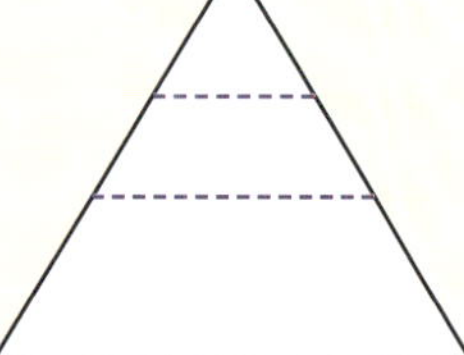

Yes/No (No circled)

How do you know?

Each part is a different size.

Shade $\frac{1}{10}$ of this rectangle.

How do you know you have shaded $\frac{1}{10}$?

Because there are 10 equal parts.

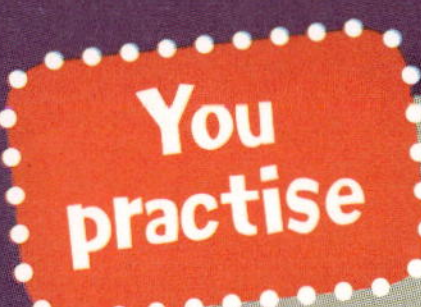

Write each shaded fraction in words and in numbers.

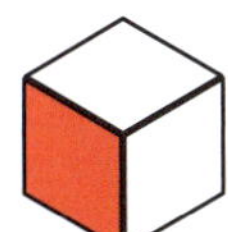

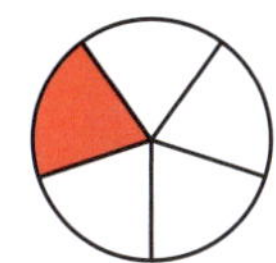

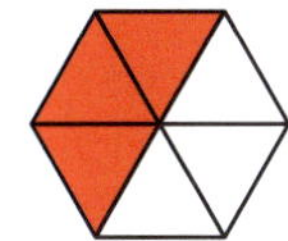

You practise

Match the fraction name, fraction and shape.

fifth $\frac{1}{6}$

third $\frac{1}{10}$

sixth $\frac{1}{5}$

tenth $\frac{2}{3}$

two thirds $\frac{1}{3}$

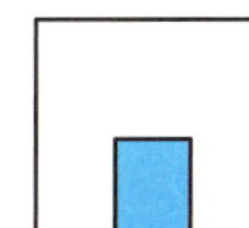

BOB time!

MORE FRACTIONS OF SHAPES

What fraction of this circle is shaded?

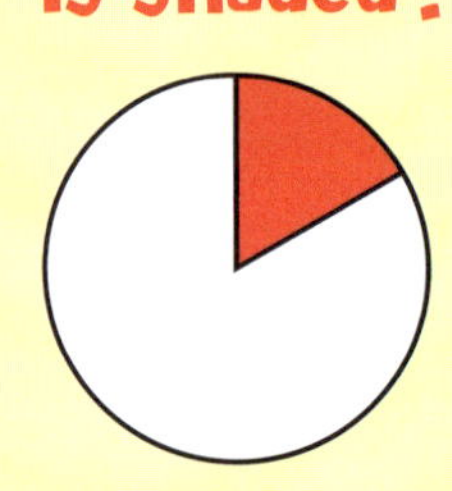

Look at the steps to find out.

Step 1

Continue the lines along each side of the shaded part.

Step 2

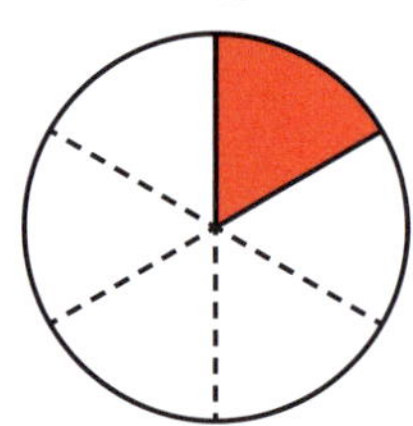

Only one more line is needed to make all equal parts.

Each part is one out of **6 equal-sized parts**.
Each part is a **sixth** ($\frac{1}{6}$).

Look at these steps to find what fraction of this rectangle is shaded.

Step 1

Step 2

You can see that there are **10 equal-sized parts**, so each is one out of ten parts or $\frac{1}{10}$.

We practise

What fraction of the L shape is this piece?

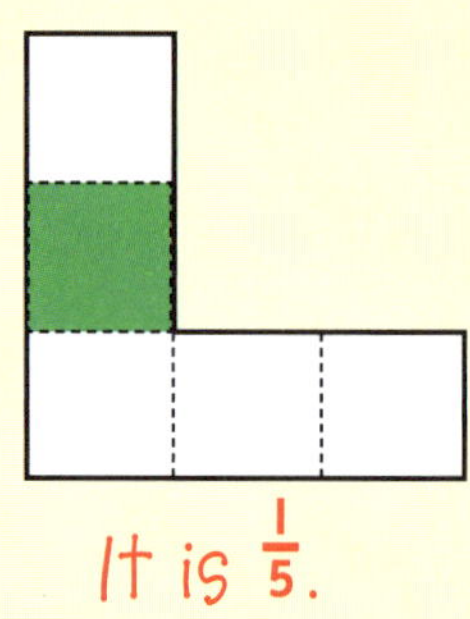

It is $\frac{1}{5}$.

What fraction of the hexagon is this piece?

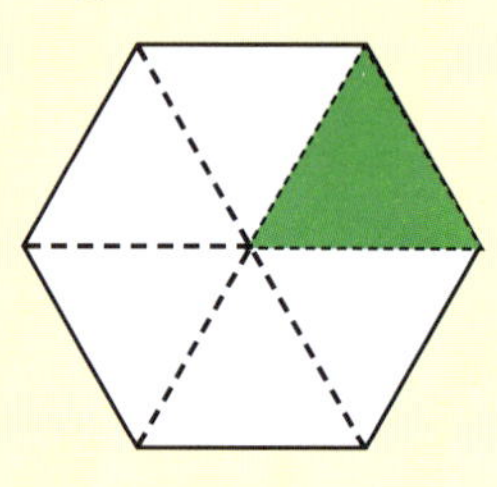

It is $\frac{1}{6}$.

Match the fraction pieces to the shapes that they were made from.

$\frac{1}{3}$

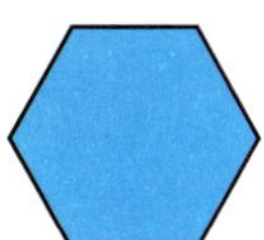

$\frac{1}{6}$

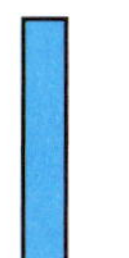

$\frac{1}{5}$

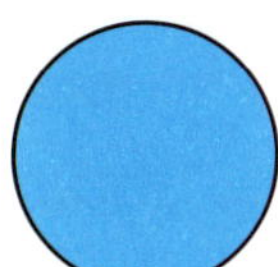

$\frac{1}{10}$

What fraction of each shape is shaded?

5

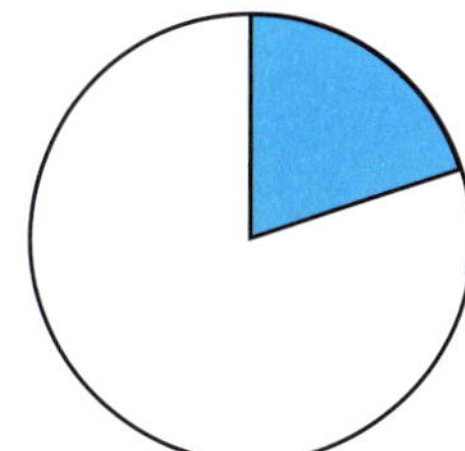

6

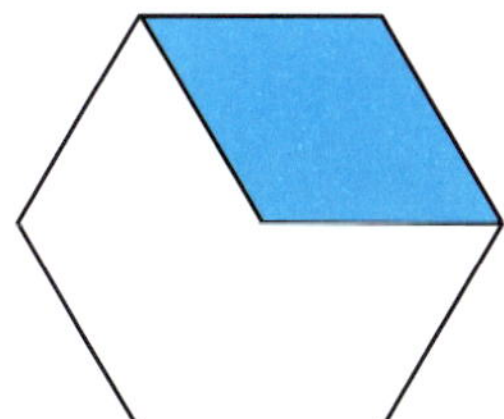

7

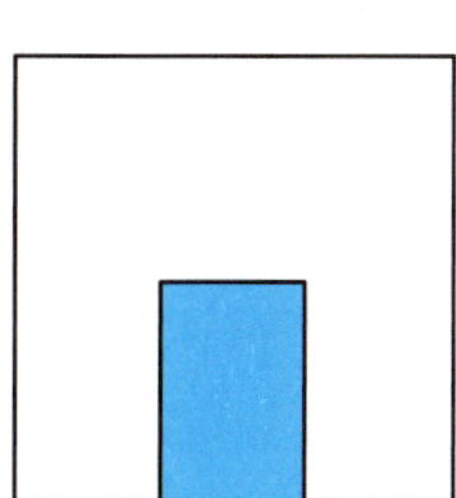

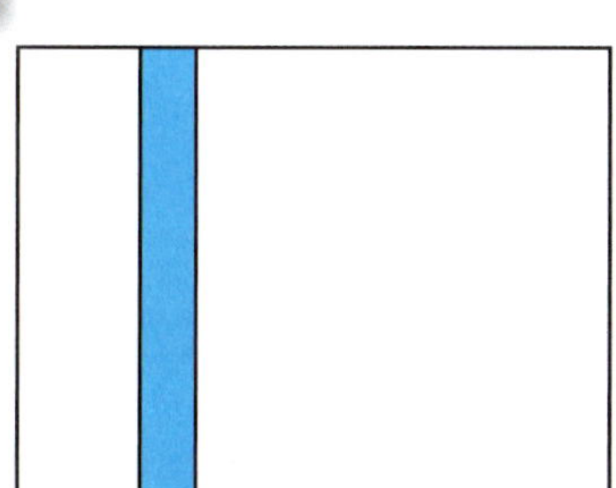

9

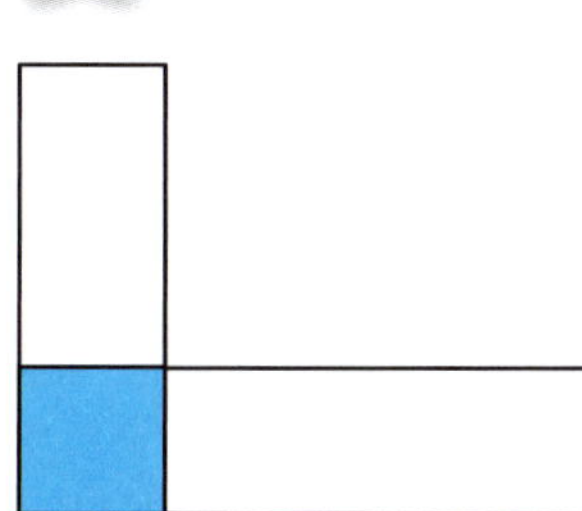

10

BOB time!

UNIT 13

MORE COUNTING in MIXED FRACTIONS

Counting in thirds and sixths or in fifths and tenths is similar to the fraction counting that you did in Unit 6, page 16.

Here are three whole rectangles that have been folded into thirds.

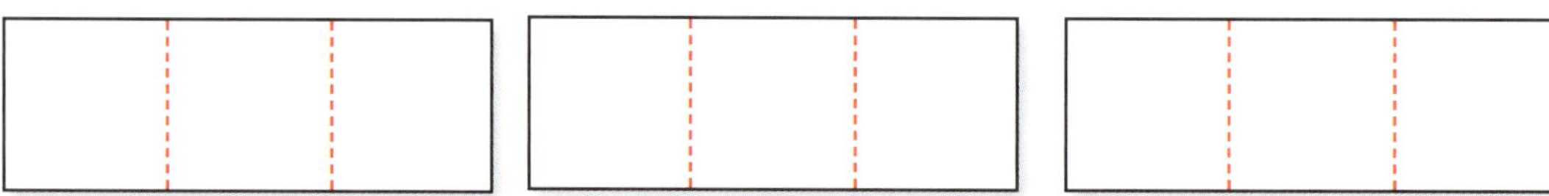

You can count the thirds: $\frac{1}{3}$, $\frac{2}{3}$, $\frac{3}{3}$, $\frac{4}{3}$… until you come to nine thirds ($\frac{9}{3}$). Then you can fold the rectangles again to make sixths and then count the sixths too (as you can see below).

$\frac{1}{6}$	$\frac{2}{6}$	$\frac{3}{6}$	$\frac{4}{6}$	$\frac{5}{6}$	$\frac{6}{6}$

$\frac{7}{6}$	$\frac{8}{6}$	$\frac{9}{6}$	$\frac{10}{6}$	$\frac{11}{6}$	$\frac{12}{6}$

$\frac{13}{6}$	$\frac{14}{6}$	$\frac{15}{6}$	$\frac{16}{6}$	$\frac{17}{6}$	$\frac{18}{6}$

To make things more interesting, you can use mixed fractions and equivalent fractions.

So let's count the sixths again and have some fun.

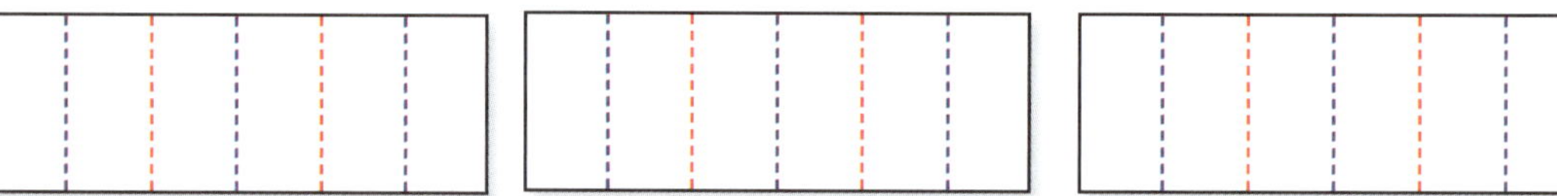

$\frac{1}{6}$, $\frac{2}{6}$, $\frac{1}{2}$, $\frac{4}{6}$, $\frac{5}{6}$, 1 $1\frac{1}{6}$, $1\frac{2}{6}$ … you carry on.

We practise

How many fifths are shaded? Count in fifths to find out.

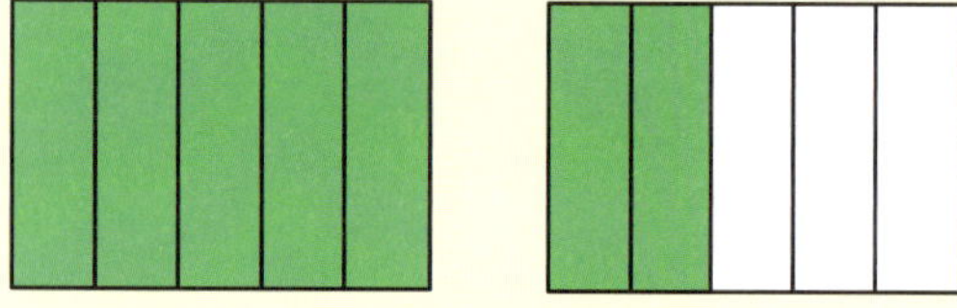

There are seven fifths, $\frac{7}{5}$.

How many tenths are shaded? Count in tenths to find out.

There are **17** tenths, which is the same as $1\frac{7}{10}$.

You practise

How many fractions are shaded?
Write the answer in words and mixed fractions.

 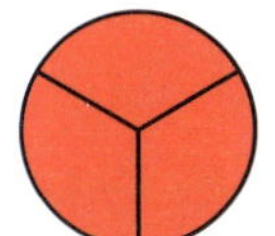 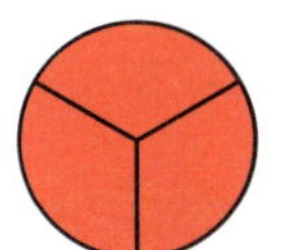 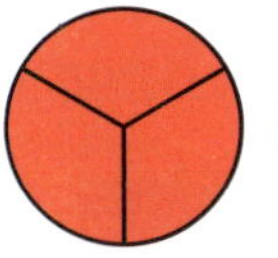 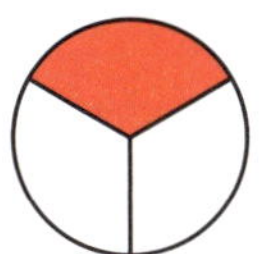 ______ thirds or ______

 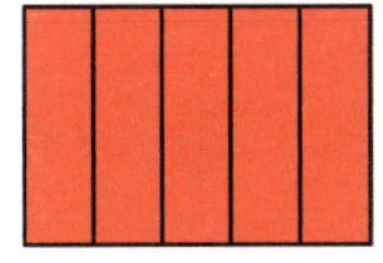  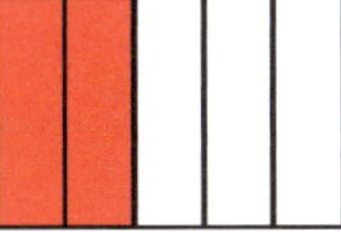 ______ fifths or ______

 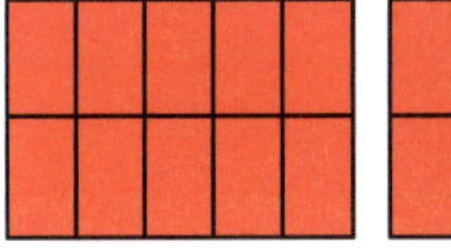  ______ tenths or ______

 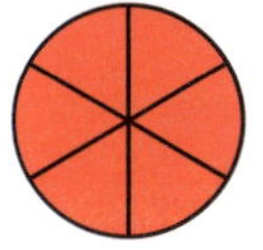 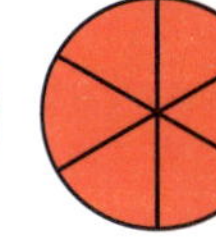 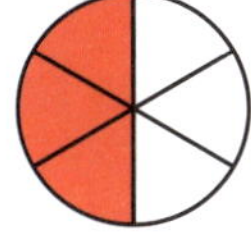  ______ sixths or ______

 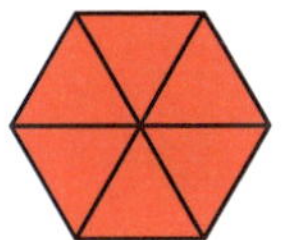 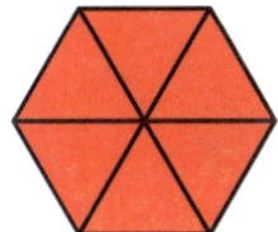 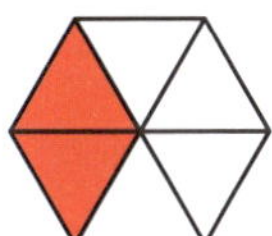 ______ sixths or ______

Remember to find out what fraction to count in by counting the number of parts in each shape.

You practise

Count and shade each fraction.

 $\frac{14}{5}$   

 $\frac{13}{6}$ 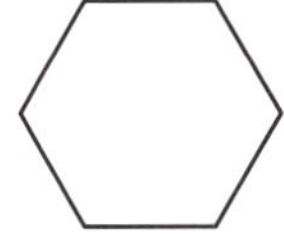 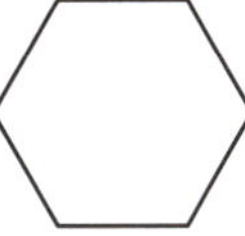  

 $\frac{23}{10}$   

 $\frac{8}{3}$   

 $\frac{13}{5}$   

Don't forget to draw in the fraction lines.

BOB time!

MORE FRACTIONS OF COLLECTIONS

To find a sixth ($\frac{1}{6}$) of 18 objects you just have to share 18 objects into 6 groups.

Another way of saying this is: 18 divided by 6.

18 divided by 6 can be written as a fraction like this: $\frac{18}{6}$.

The diagram shows 18 objects shared equally into 6 groups. Each is a $\frac{1}{6}$ of 18.

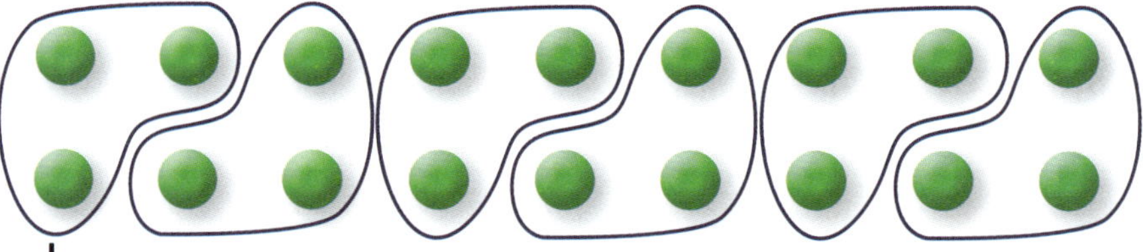

$\frac{1}{6}$ of 18 equals 3

What if you are asked to find $\frac{5}{6}$ of 18 objects?

Circle five of the groups ($\frac{5}{6}$) to find the answer.

There are 5 groups of 3, so the answer is 15.

If you know that $\frac{3}{4}$ of a collection is 9 objects, then how do you find out how many in the collection altogether?

Draw four spaces, one for each quarter. Then share 9 counters equally into 3 of the quarters.

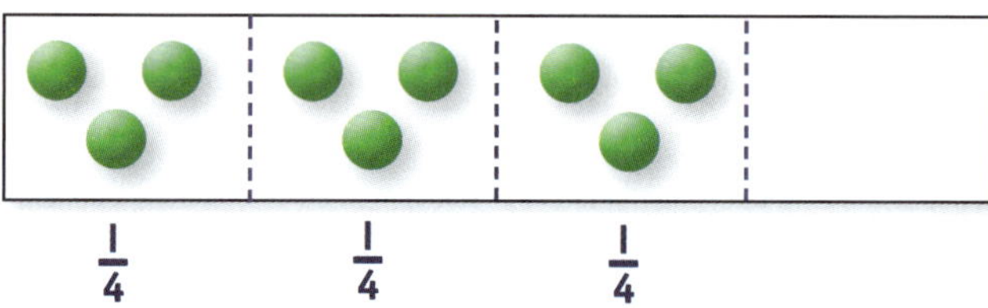

Now you can see that $\frac{1}{4}$ equals 3 objects. 4 quarters would be 4 lots of 3, so the answer is 12.

What is $\frac{2}{3}$ of 9 marbles? Draw a picture to show how to work this out.

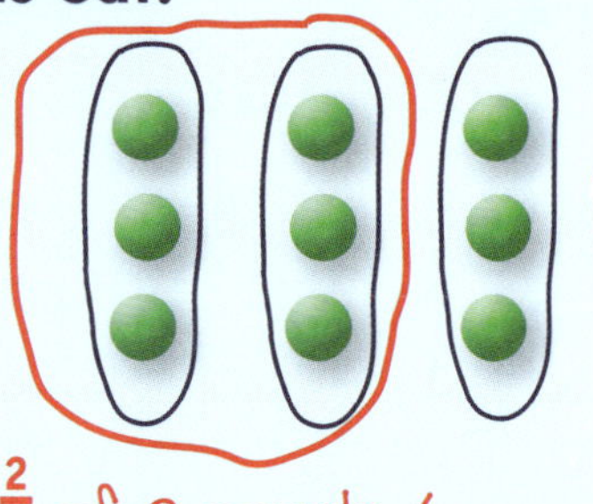

We practise

$\frac{2}{3}$ of 9 equals 6.

How many in the collection altogether if $\frac{3}{4}$ of the collection is 6? Draw a picture to show how to work this out.

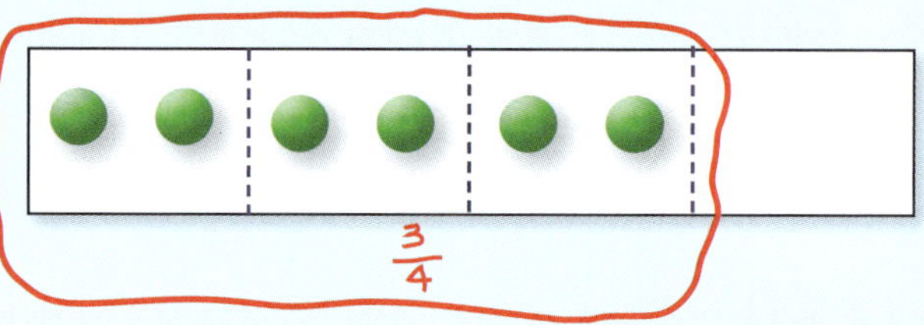

There are 8 in the collection altogether.

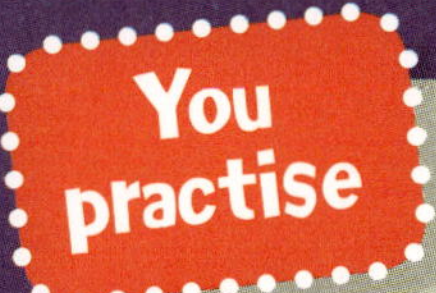

Show how to work out each fraction of these collections and write the answer.

 1  

$\frac{2}{3}$ of ______ equals ______

 2   

$\frac{2}{5}$ of ______ equals ______

 3   

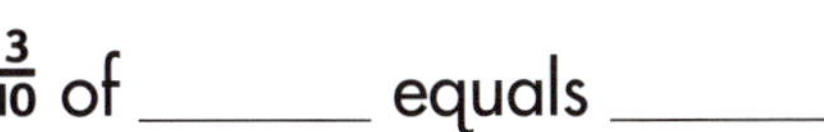

$\frac{3}{10}$ of ______ equals ______

 4      

$\frac{4}{6}$ of ______ equals ______

 5       

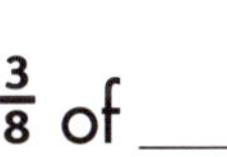

$\frac{3}{8}$ of ______ equals ______

You practise

How many objects are in each collection?

 6 $\frac{1}{2}$ of the collection is 4.
There are ______ in the collection.

  7 $\frac{1}{4}$ of the collection is 4.
There are ______ in the collection.

8 $\frac{1}{5}$ of the collection is 2.
There are ______ in the collection.

 9 $\frac{2}{5}$ of the collection is 4.
There are ______ in the collection.

 10 $\frac{1}{10}$ of the collection is 2.
There are ______ in the collection.

Remember, drawing pictures might help with this.

FRACTION WALLS

This is a **fraction wall**. It shows the sizes of the fractions.

A fraction wall can be used to find equivalent fractions or to compare fractions.

$\frac{1}{2}$	$\frac{1}{2}$								
$\frac{1}{4}$	$\frac{1}{4}$	$\frac{1}{4}$	$\frac{1}{4}$						
$\frac{1}{8}$	$\frac{1}{8}$	$\frac{1}{8}$	$\frac{1}{8}$	$\frac{1}{8}$	$\frac{1}{8}$	$\frac{1}{8}$	$\frac{1}{8}$		
$\frac{1}{3}$	$\frac{1}{3}$	$\frac{1}{3}$							
$\frac{1}{6}$	$\frac{1}{6}$	$\frac{1}{6}$	$\frac{1}{6}$	$\frac{1}{6}$	$\frac{1}{6}$				
$\frac{1}{5}$	$\frac{1}{5}$	$\frac{1}{5}$	$\frac{1}{5}$	$\frac{1}{5}$					
$\frac{1}{10}$	$\frac{1}{10}$	$\frac{1}{10}$	$\frac{1}{10}$	$\frac{1}{10}$	$\frac{1}{10}$	$\frac{1}{10}$	$\frac{1}{10}$	$\frac{1}{10}$	$\frac{1}{10}$

There is a line right down the middle of the fraction wall to show the **benchmark fraction** $\frac{1}{2}$. It is called a benchmark because it is useful for comparing fractions and later for adding fractions.

Find the sixths on the wall and count along 3 sixths and you will notice that $\frac{3}{6}$ is equivalent to $\frac{1}{2}$.

Find $\frac{3}{5}$ on the wall and use the benchmark (halfway line) to see if it is smaller or larger than $\frac{1}{2}$.

We practise

Use the fraction wall to find out whether $\frac{3}{5}$ or $\frac{3}{8}$ is closer to $\frac{1}{2}$.

$\frac{3}{5}$ is closer to $\frac{1}{2}$.

Use the fraction wall to find out if $\frac{5}{8}$ or $\frac{3}{4}$ is closer to 1.

$\frac{3}{4}$ is closer to 1.

You practise

Which fraction is closer to $\frac{1}{2}$?

$\frac{1}{5}$ or $\frac{1}{8}$ ____ is closer.

Remember to use the fraction wall.

$\frac{2}{5}$ or $\frac{4}{6}$ ____ is closer.

$\frac{4}{5}$ or $\frac{4}{10}$ ____ is closer.

$\frac{3}{8}$ or $\frac{2}{5}$ ____ is closer.

$\frac{5}{8}$ or $\frac{7}{6}$ ____ is closer.

Which fraction is closer to 1?

$\frac{3}{8}$ or $\frac{1}{4}$ ____ is closer.

$\frac{3}{10}$ or $\frac{2}{5}$ ____ is closer.

$\frac{4}{5}$ or $\frac{5}{8}$ ____ is closer.

$\frac{5}{6}$ or $\frac{5}{8}$ ____ is closer.

$\frac{1}{3}$ or $\frac{1}{4}$ ____ is closer.

UNIT 16 MORE EQUIVALENT FRACTIONS

You have already learnt that $\frac{4}{8}$ is equivalent to $\frac{2}{4}$ (Unit 8, page 20).
Now you can learn about other **equivalent fractions**.

Sixths and thirds, sixths and halves, fifths and tenths, tenths and halves are easy to work with too.

This diagram shows that $\frac{3}{6}$ is equivalent to $\frac{1}{2}$.

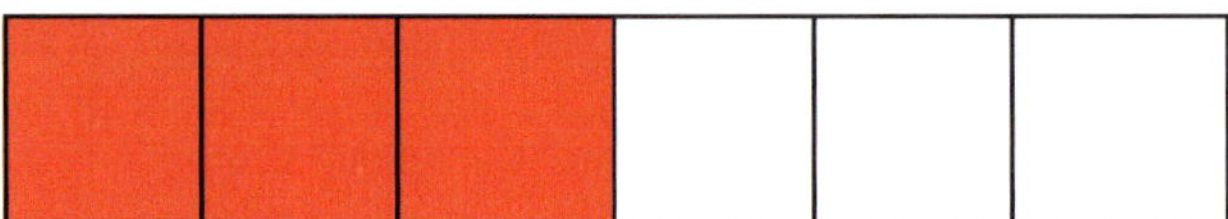

This diagram shows that $\frac{2}{6}$ is equivalent to $\frac{1}{3}$.

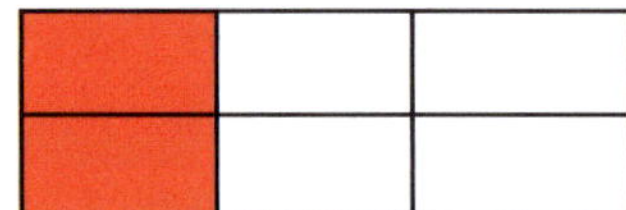

This diagram shows that $\frac{5}{10}$ is equivalent to $\frac{1}{2}$.

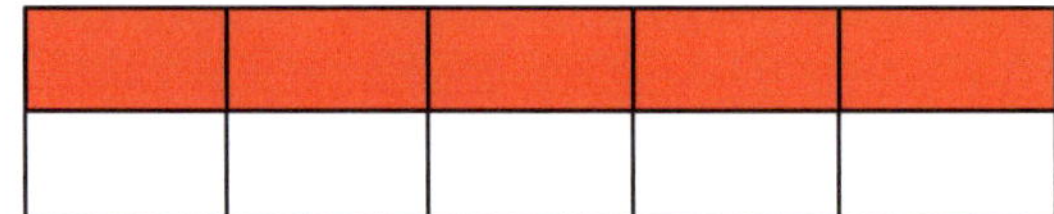

This diagram shows that $\frac{2}{10}$ is equivalent to $\frac{1}{5}$.

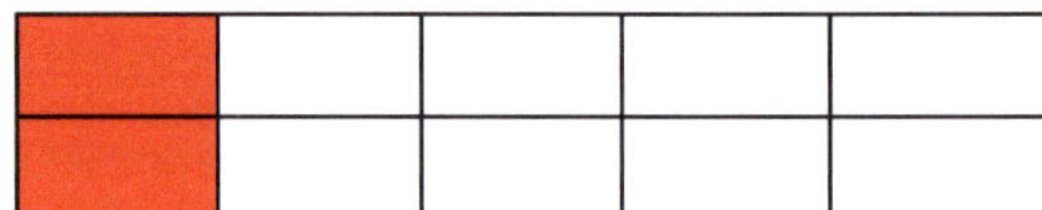

We practise

Draw a diagram to show how many tenths are equivalent to $\frac{4}{5}$.

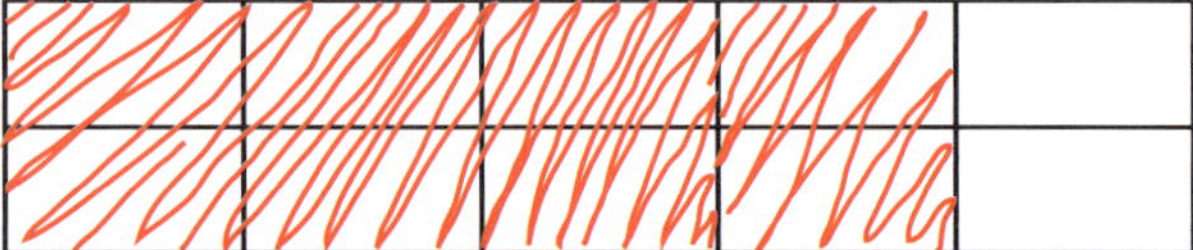

$\frac{8}{10}$ is equivalent to $\frac{4}{5}$.

$\frac{4}{6}$ plus how many more sixths equals 1?

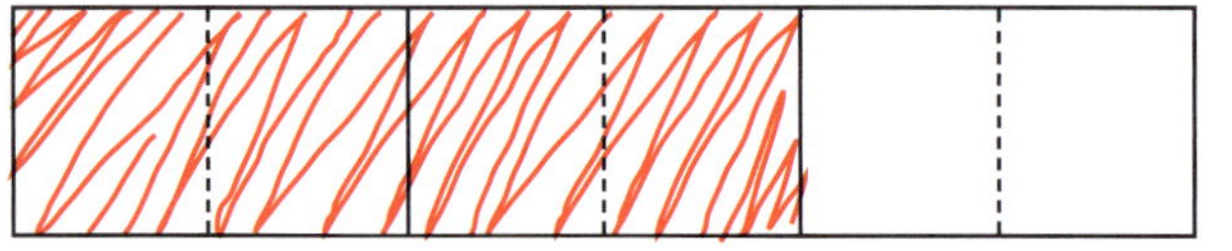

$\frac{2}{6}$

You practise

Complete the equivalent fraction sentences.

1. $\frac{3}{6}$ is equivalent to 

2. $\frac{5}{10}$ is equivalent to 

3. $\frac{4}{10}$ is equivalent to 

4. $\frac{4}{6}$ is equivalent to 

5. $\frac{2}{5}$ is equivalent to 

Remember to use the fraction wall or draw diagrams.

You practise

Complete the equivalent fraction sentences.

6. $\frac{1}{6}$ plus ______ is equivalent to $\frac{1}{2}$

7. $\frac{1}{8}$ plus ______ is equivalent to $\frac{1}{2}$

8. $\frac{4}{10}$ plus ______ is equivalent to $\frac{1}{2}$

9. $\frac{3}{5}$ plus ______ is equivalent to 1

10. $\frac{1}{4}$ plus ______ is equivalent to $\frac{1}{2}$

The fraction wall or drawing diagrams could also help.

BOB time!

ADDING FRACTIONS

People can make silly mistakes when adding fractions.

Here is $\frac{1}{2}$ a pizza.

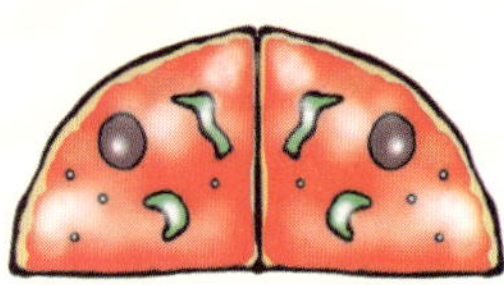

Here is $\frac{1}{4}$ of a pizza.

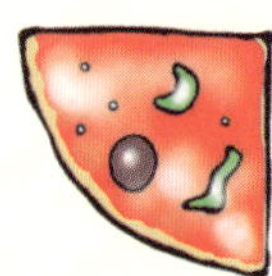

If you put the two pieces together, you can see that $\frac{1}{2} + \frac{1}{4}$ is the same as $\frac{3}{4}$.

It is important to stop and think about the answer to a question such as $\frac{1}{2} + \frac{1}{4}$.

If you write the fraction sum down and then add the top numbers (numerators) together and then add the bottom two numbers (denominators) together, you will get the silly answer shown below.

$\frac{1}{2} + \frac{1}{4} = \frac{2}{6}$ This cannot be right!

Why is the answer silly? Because if you add another fraction to a half, then the answer will be larger than a half. $\frac{2}{6}$ is smaller than $\frac{1}{2}$, so it cannot be correct.

This number line shows $\frac{1}{2} + \frac{1}{4}$.

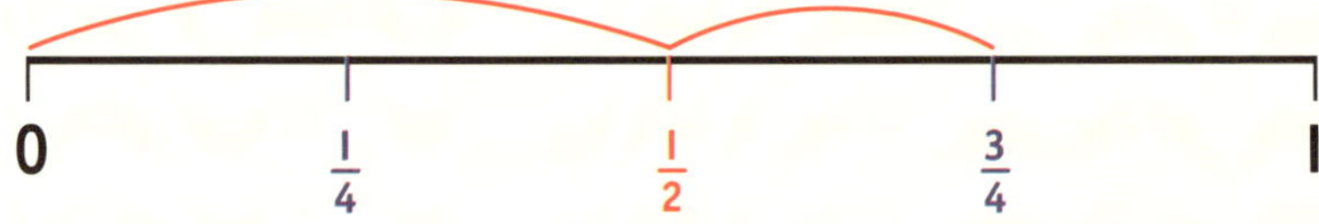

This number line shows what $\frac{2}{6}$ looks like. Do you see the difference?

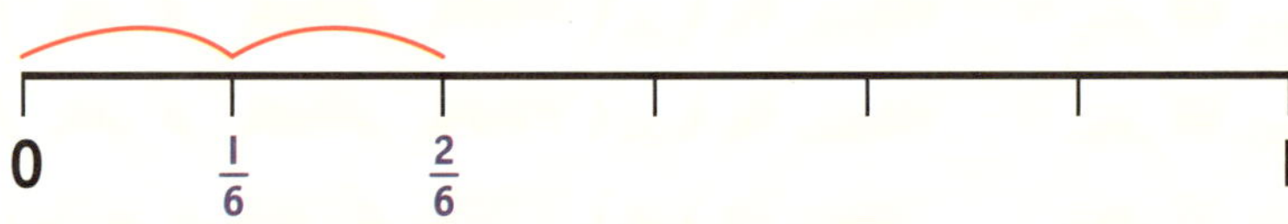

We practise

Use a number line to find if $\frac{1}{4} + \frac{1}{4}$ is more than, less than or the same as $\frac{1}{2}$.

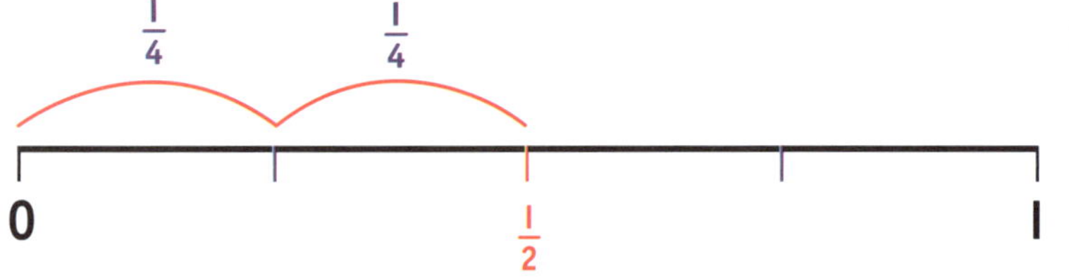

$\frac{1}{4} + \frac{1}{4}$ more less same

Use a number line to show the answer to $\frac{3}{6} + \frac{1}{6}$.

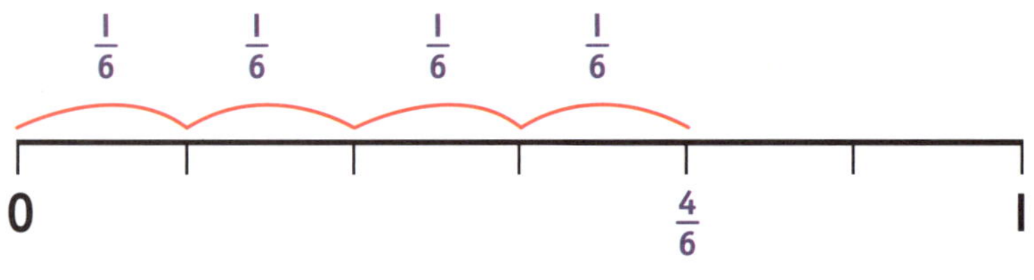

$\frac{3}{6} + \frac{1}{6} = \frac{4}{6}$ or $\frac{2}{3}$

You practise

Is the answer more than, less than or the same as $\frac{1}{2}$? Use a number line to work out the answer.

1. $\frac{1}{2} + \frac{1}{6}$ more less same

2. $\frac{1}{3} + \frac{1}{6}$ more less same

3. $\frac{2}{5} + \frac{1}{5}$ more less same

4. $\frac{3}{8} + \frac{2}{8}$ more less same

5. $\frac{6}{10} + \frac{3}{10}$ more less same

Remember to use the fraction wall.

You practise

Think about equivalent fractions to work out these additions. Use a number line to work out each answer.

6. $\frac{1}{8} + \frac{1}{4} =$ ______

7. $\frac{1}{3} + \frac{1}{6} =$ ______

8. $\frac{1}{2} + \frac{1}{8} =$ ______

9. $\frac{2}{5} + \frac{1}{10} =$ ______ 0

10. $\frac{1}{2} + \frac{1}{6} =$ ______ 0

BOB time!

MEETING DECIMALS

A tenth is a decimal fraction and so is a hundredth. Decimals work in multiples of ten in a similar way to whole numbers except that a tenth is smaller than 1 whole and a hundredth is smaller than a tenth.

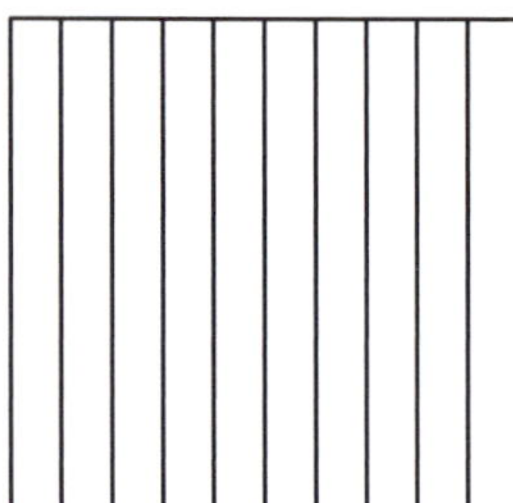

To show you how this works, here is one square that has been cut into 10 smaller parts. Each part is called a tenth.

As a second example, here are two whole squares that have been shaded. The shading shows the decimal number that equals 1 and $\frac{3}{10}$. This is written as $1\frac{3}{10}$.

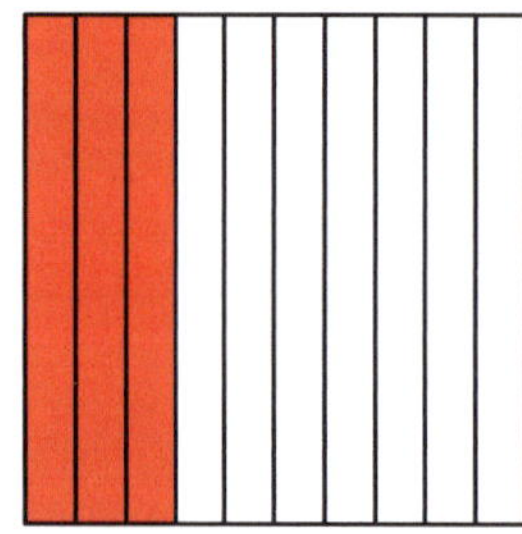

Decimal numbers are written differently to fractions. The whole number is written first and then a decimal point separates the whole number from the fraction part.

For example, 1·3, which you can say as **one point three** or as **one and three tenths**.

We practise

Write the decimal number to match this diagram as a decimal and as a mixed fraction.

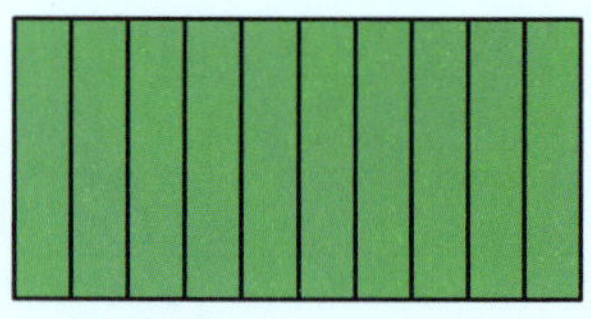

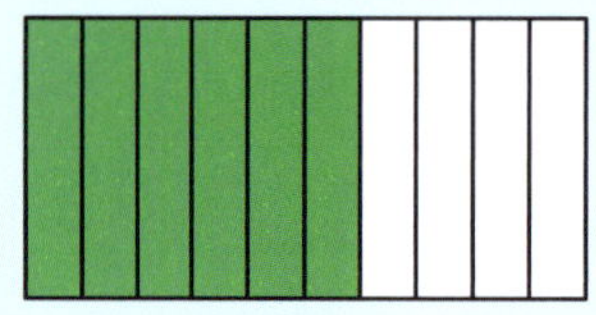

1·6, $\frac{16}{10}$

Shade this diagram to match the decimal fraction 0·5.

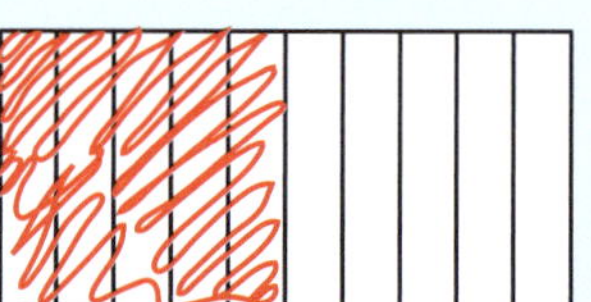

You practise

Write the decimal and fraction that match each diagram.

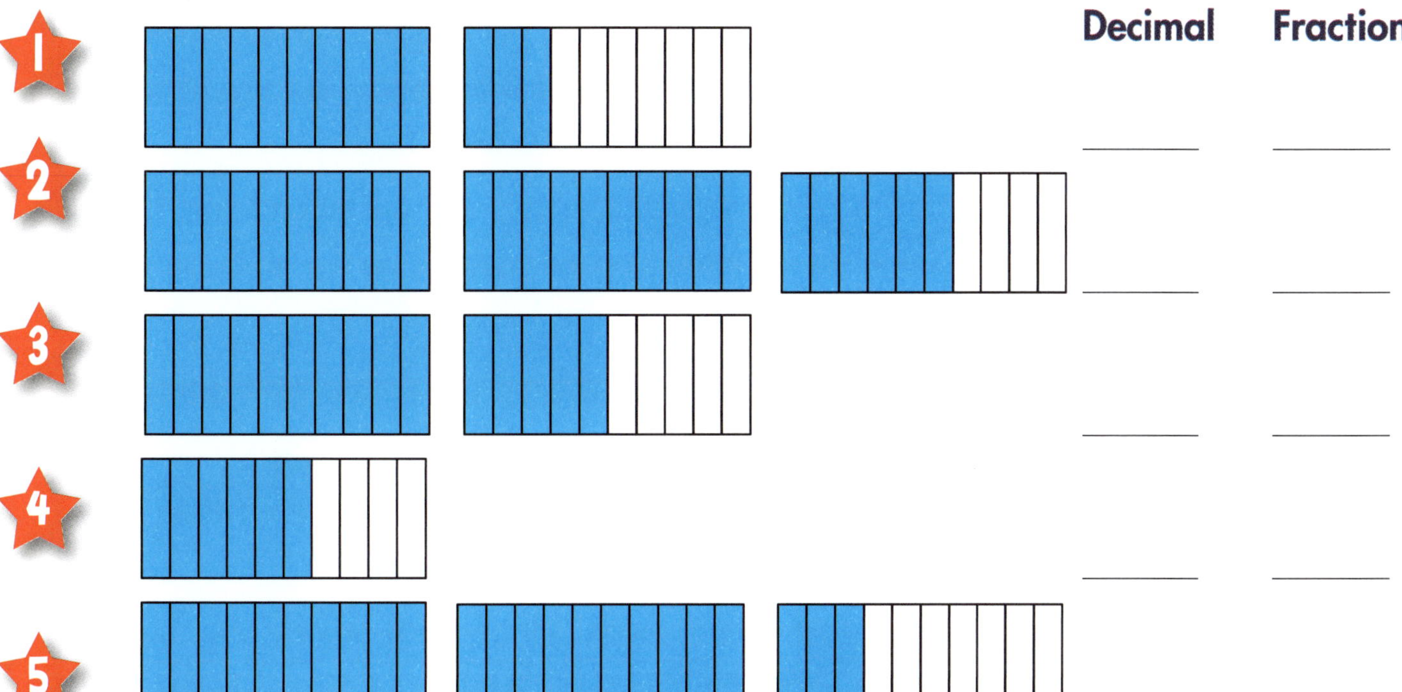

You practise

Shade the diagrams to match the decimal numbers.

 1·3  

 2·3 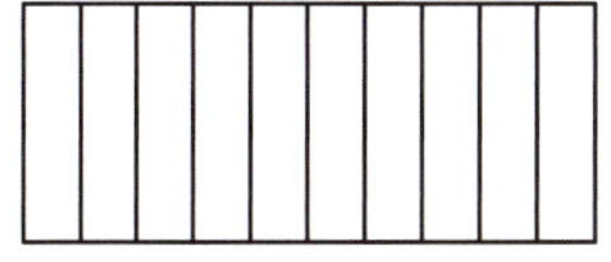 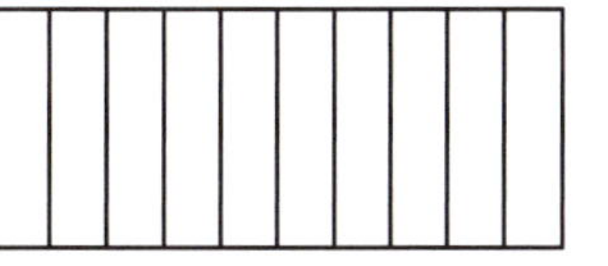 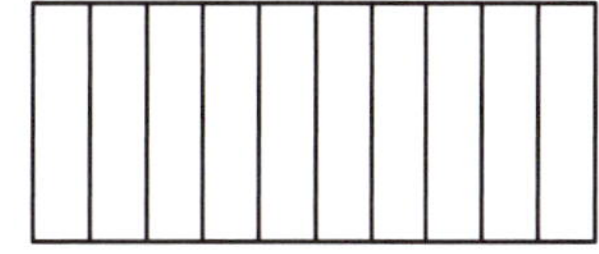

 2·4  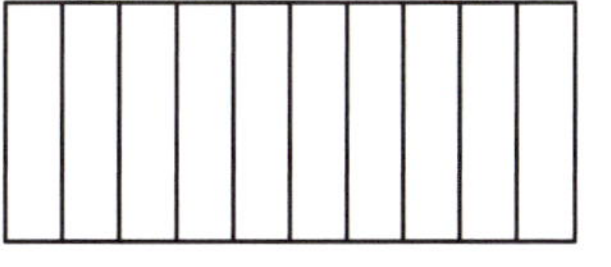 

 2·6   

 0·5 

BOB time!

DECIMALS TO HUNDREDTHS

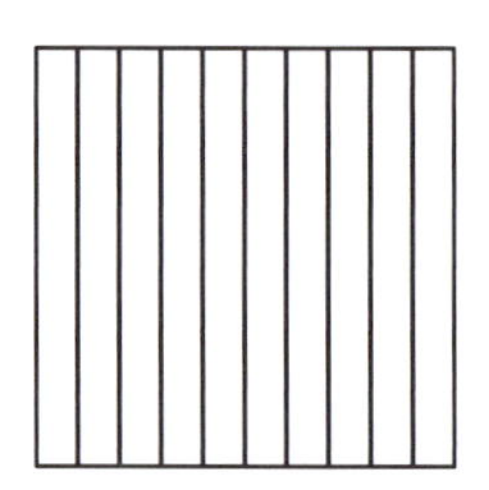

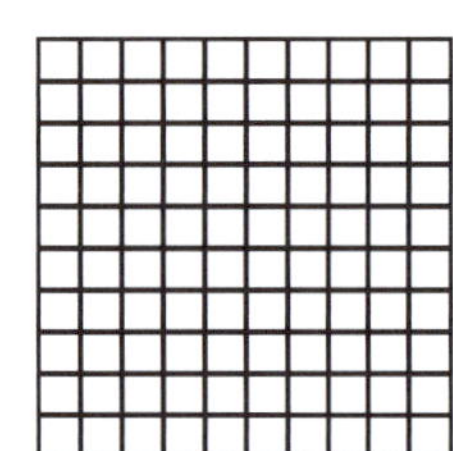

Hundredths are a lot smaller than tenths. Here is square cut into tenths and next to it a square cut into hundredths.

Look carefully and you will see that it takes 10 of the little hundredths to fill up the tenth, so $\frac{10}{100}$ is equivalent to $\frac{1}{10}$.

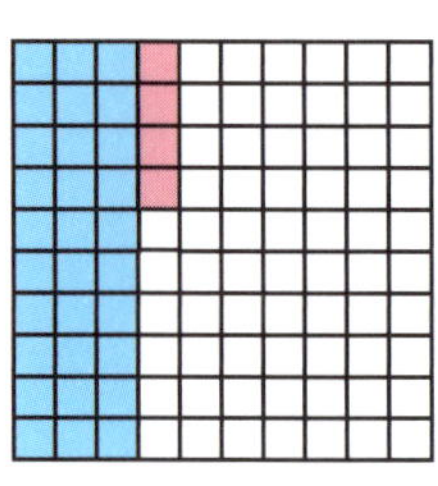

0·34 or $\frac{34}{100}$

This square has been shaded to show 34 hundredths and its decimal number and fraction number are written underneath.

You could count each one of those little squares one by one, but there is an easier way. The blue shading shows $\frac{3}{10}$ and the pink shading shows $\frac{4}{100}$. You know that $\frac{10}{100}$ are equivalent to $\frac{1}{10}$, so $\frac{3}{10}$ will be equivalent to $\frac{30}{100}$.

$\frac{34}{100}$ can be written as a decimal.
You need a zero in the ones position so that you know there are no whole numbers. The decimal point separates the part numbers from the whole numbers. You write the tenths first, and there are 3 of them, so that's 0·3. The hundredths are written next, and there are four of them, so the decimal is 0·34.

We practise

Write the decimal number for this diagram.

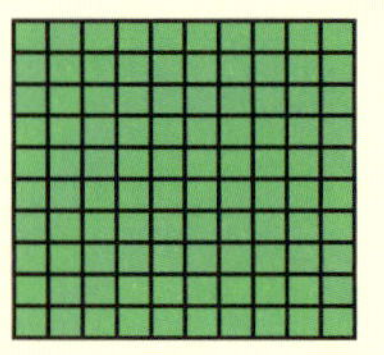

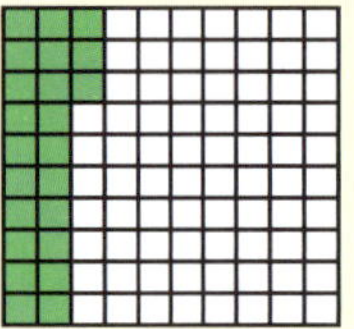

1·23

Shade the diagrams to match 1·56.

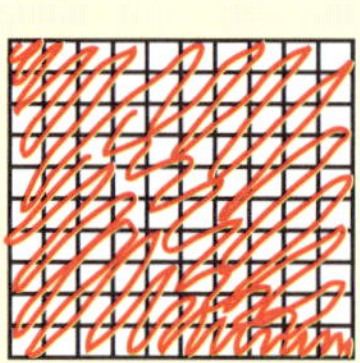

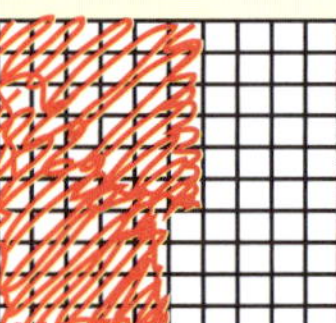

You practise

Write the decimals numbers to match the diagrams.

1

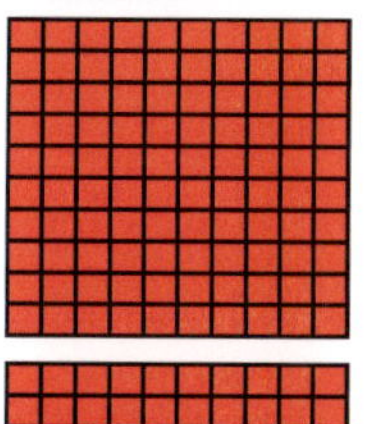

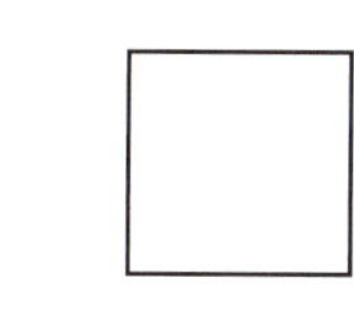

2

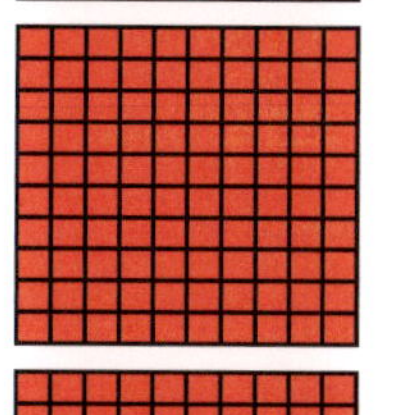
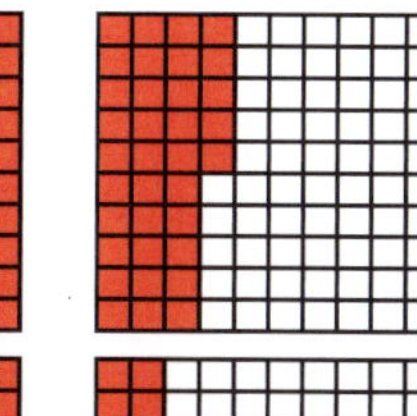

3

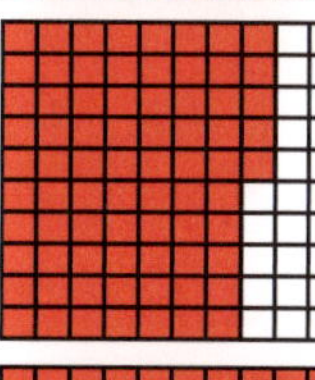

4

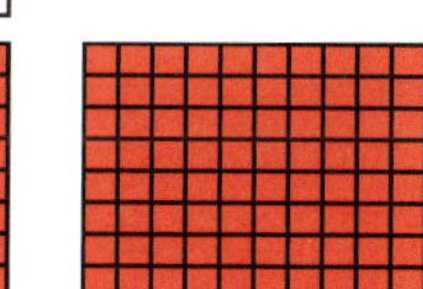

5

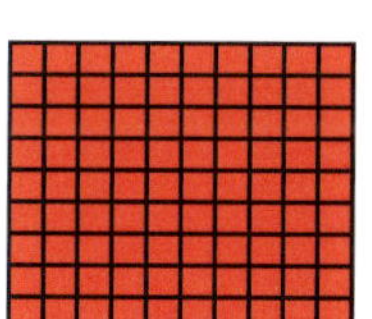
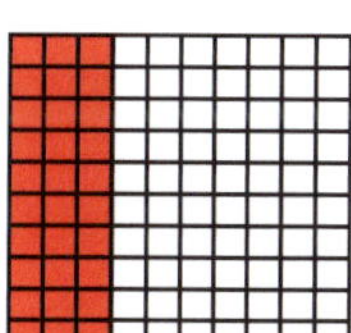

You practise

Shade the diagrams to match the decimal numbers.

6 2·4

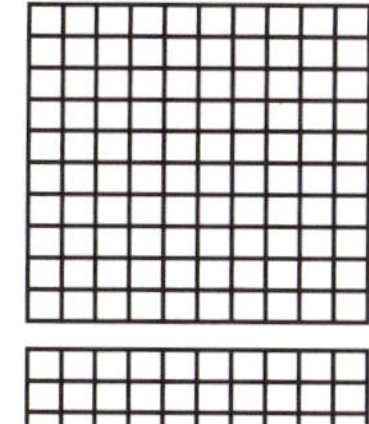
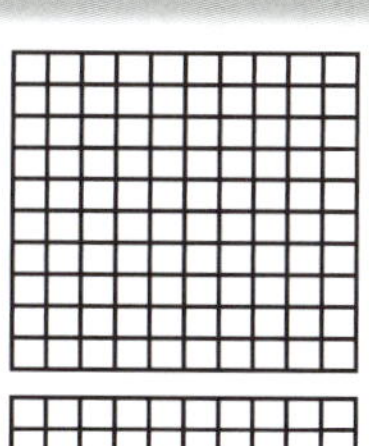
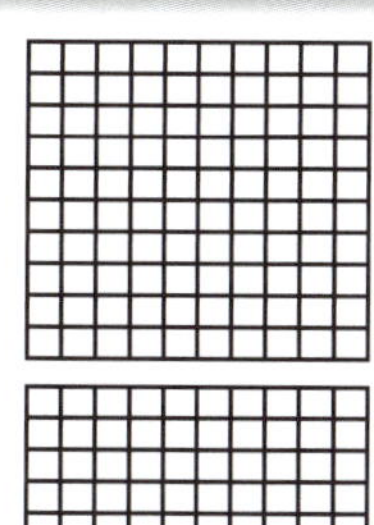

7 2·86

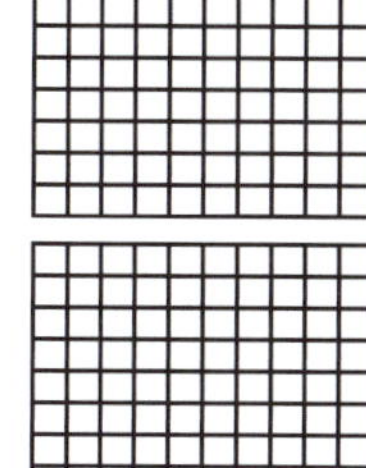
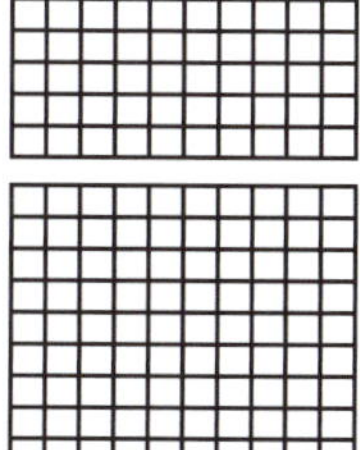

8 1·75

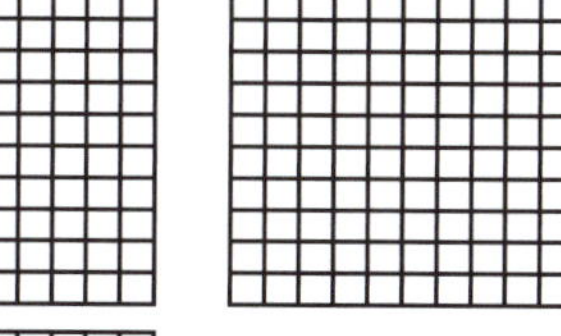

9 0·85

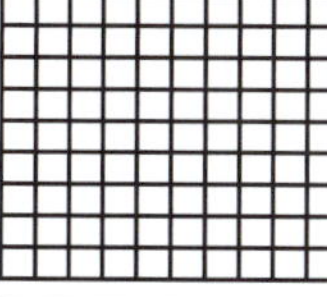

10 1·05

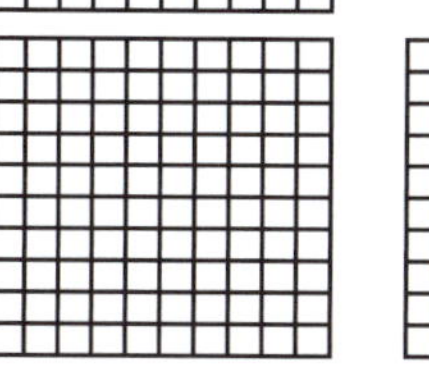
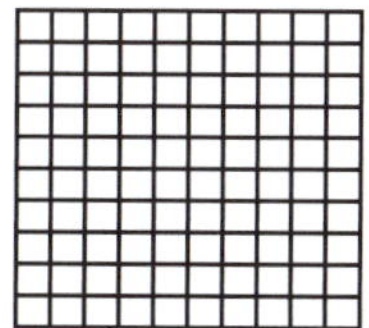

BOB time!

PROBLEM SOLVING

A Fraction Problem

Storm and Max are playing a game called 'fill the grid'. These are the playing grids they used.

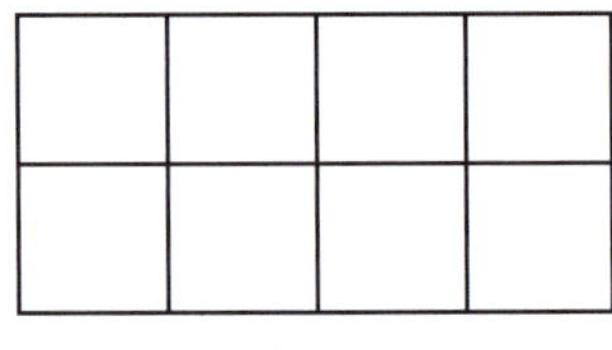

Storm

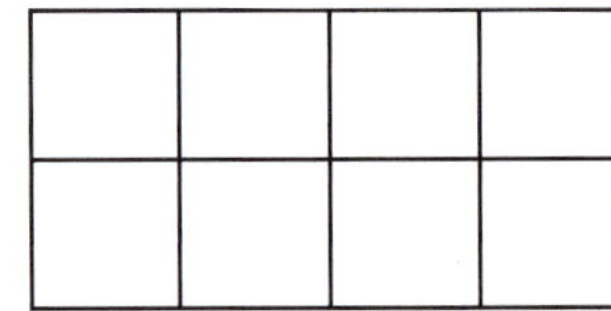

Max

They have a fraction dice marked with $\frac{1}{2}$, $\frac{1}{4}$, $\frac{3}{4}$, $\frac{1}{8}$, $\frac{3}{8}$ and $\frac{5}{8}$.

Storm threw: $\frac{1}{4}$, $\frac{1}{2}$ and $\frac{1}{8}$.

Max threw: $\frac{3}{8}$, $\frac{1}{4}$ and $\frac{1}{8}$.

Who is closer to filling their grid?

Who's winning – Max or Storm?

Notice the important information is highlighted in blue and what has to be found out is highlighted in pink. Drawing a diagram and filling up the grids helps to solve this problem.

Look how each throw is shaded on the grids opposite.

We practise

Highlight the important information and what you have to find out.

Who is closer to filling their grid?

Storm threw $\frac{1}{4}$, $\frac{1}{2}$ and $\frac{1}{8}$.

Storm

Max threw $\frac{3}{8}$, $\frac{1}{4}$ and $\frac{1}{8}$.

Max

Storm is closer to filling the grid than Max.

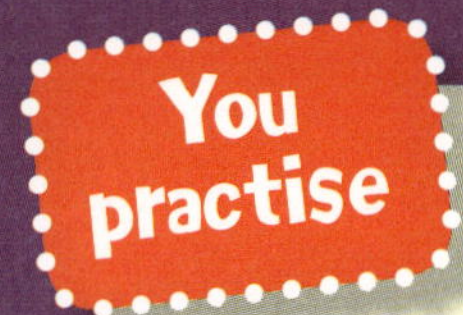

Highlight the important information and solve the problems.

1. Storm threw $\frac{1}{8}$, $\frac{1}{4}$ and $\frac{1}{2}$. Max threw $\frac{1}{4}$, $\frac{1}{4}$ and $\frac{3}{8}$.
   Who is closer to a score of 1, Storm or Max? ____________________

2. The 24 collector cards were sorted into matching sets. $\frac{1}{3}$ of them are V8 super cars, $\frac{1}{4}$ of them are vintage cars and the rest are racing cars. How many racing cars are there? __________

3. Max spent $\frac{1}{10}$ of his money on a present for Storm. He has \$90 left. How much money did Max start with? __________

4. Storm downloaded 12 tunes from the iTunes store onto her new iPod. $\frac{2}{3}$ of them are by solo artists. The rest are by girl bands. How many girl band tunes did she download? __________

5. Max said that 0.5 plus $\frac{1}{2}$ equals 1. Carlos says that's not true.
   Who is right? __________

6. Storm sorted a bag of Smarties by colour. She found $\frac{1}{5}$ of them were red, $\frac{3}{10}$ of them were blue and the other 50 are yellow. How many Smarties were in the packet? __________

7. Storm and Max are arguing over decimals in their homework question: Which is larger: 0·45 or 0·6? Storm says 0·45 is larger, but Max says 0·6 is the larger. Who is correct? __________

8. "Share the three pizzas fairly between yourselves," said Mum to Max, Carlos, Storm and their friend Jo, "I want everyone to get the same."
   How should the pizzas be cut to make this possible? __________

9. "If I add $\frac{1}{6}$, $\frac{1}{3}$, $\frac{1}{2}$ and $\frac{1}{8}$, $\frac{1}{4}$, $\frac{1}{2}$, how close to 2 will my answer be?" asked Storm.
   Max said, "Very close."
   What other fraction is needed to make the answer add up to 2? __________

10. "Write the fraction $\frac{5}{10}$ in 3 different ways, including a decimal as one of the ways," said Mrs Brown. ______________

BOB time!

TEST 1

1. Show how to cut this shape into eighths.

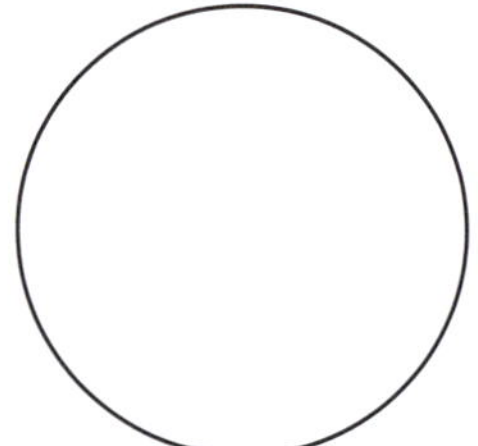

2. What fraction of this shape is shaded?

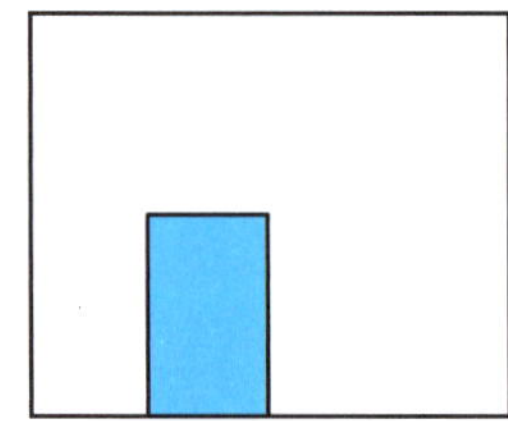

______

3. How many eighths are shaded?

______

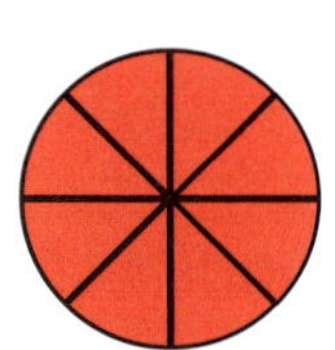 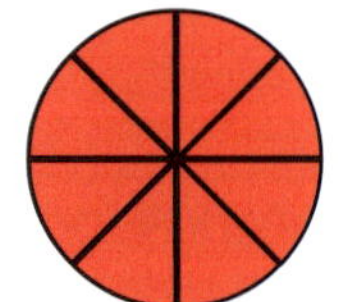 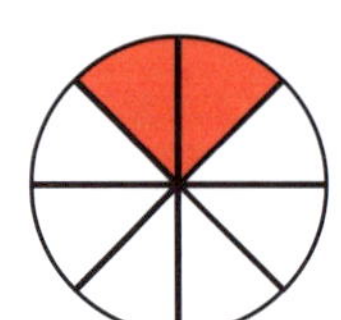

4. Share the marbles into quarters.

5. What fraction of the cookies are on each plate?

______

6. Show $\frac{3}{4}$ on the number line.

0 ———————————— 1

7. Show $\frac{7}{8}$ on the number line.

0 ———————————— 1

8. Shade the rectangles to show $1\frac{3}{4}$.

9. Use the number line to show $\frac{3}{8}$ and $\frac{3}{4}$.
Which is larger $\frac{3}{8}$ or $\frac{3}{4}$?

______

0 ———————————— 1

10. What is $\frac{6}{8}$ equivalent to? ______

TEST 2

1 What fraction of this shape is shaded? Write the fraction in words and as a fraction.

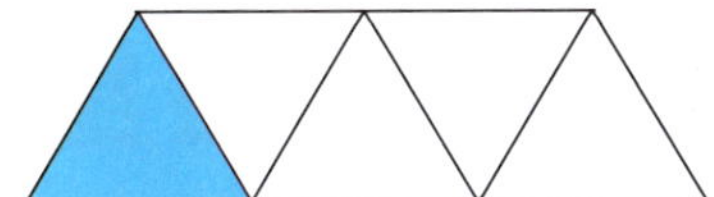

____

2 What fraction of the whole shape is shown?

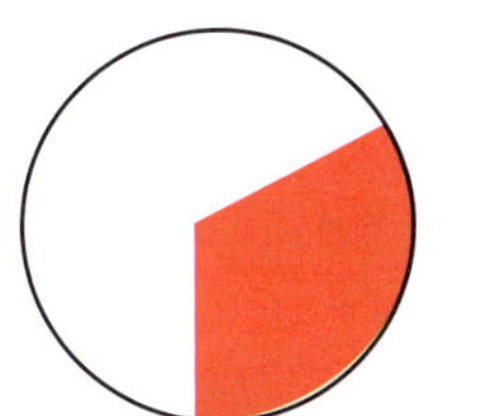

____

3 What fractional parts are used in the diagrams? How many of them are there?

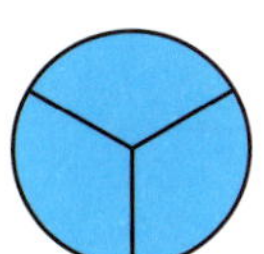 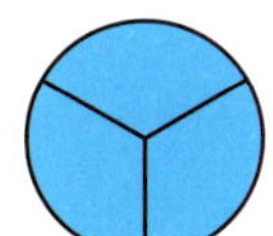 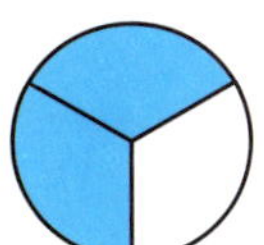

____

4 Circle $\frac{2}{3}$ of this group of marbles.

5 Show which of the fractions, $\frac{3}{8}$ and $\frac{3}{4}$, is closer to $\frac{1}{2}$ on the number line.

6 I have $\frac{5}{8}$ of a pizza left. How much has already been eaten?

____

7 Is $\frac{3}{8} + \frac{1}{4}$ more than, less than or the same as $\frac{1}{2}$?

____

8 What is $\frac{3}{8} + \frac{1}{8}$ equivalent to?

____

9 Shade 1·9 of the diagram.

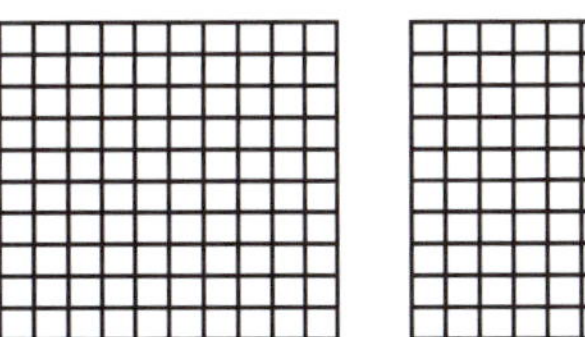

10 What decimal number is shown in the diagram?

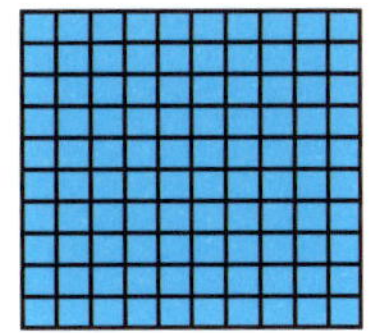 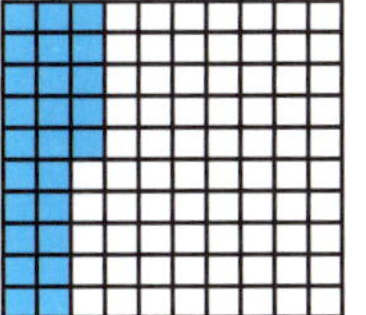

____

ANSWERS

Unit 1

1–6

7

8 – 10

eighth $\frac{1}{8}$

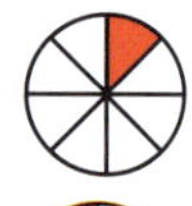

half $\frac{1}{2}$

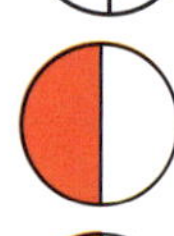

quarter $\frac{1}{4}$

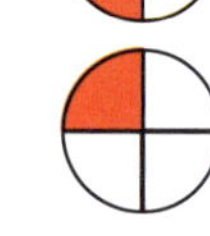

Unit 2

1 – 5

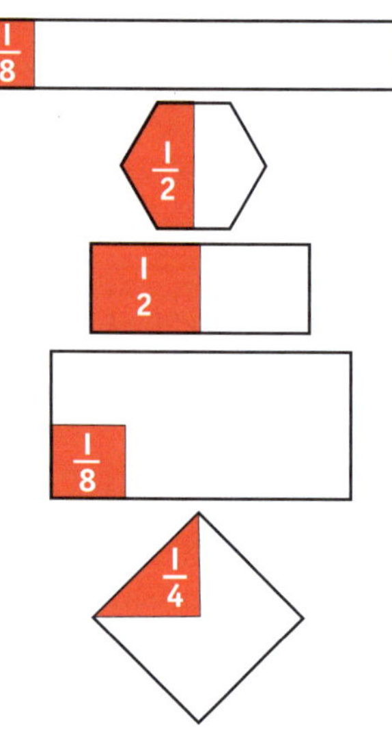

6 $\frac{1}{8}$
7 $\frac{1}{4}$
8 $\frac{1}{2}$
9 $\frac{1}{4}$
10 $\frac{1}{4}$

Unit 3

1 7 halves
2 9 quarters
3 19 eighths
4 23 eighths
5 12 eighths

6

7

8

9

10

Unit 4

1

2

3

4

5

6 Each plate has $\frac{1}{4}$ of the 12 cakes.
7 Each plate has $\frac{1}{8}$ of the 16 cakes.
8 Each plate has $\frac{1}{8}$ of the 32 cakes.
9 Each plate has $\frac{1}{2}$ of the 10 cakes.
10 Each plate has $\frac{1}{4}$ of the 24 cakes.

Unit 5

1 – 5

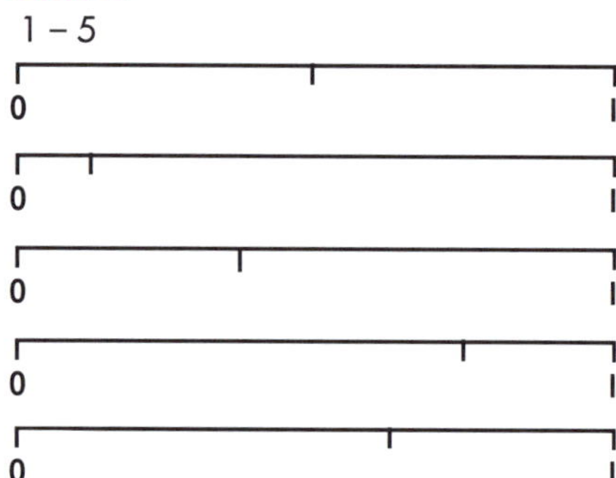

6 the fraction is $\frac{5}{8}$
7 the fraction is $\frac{3}{4}$
8 the fraction is $\frac{1}{2}$
9 the fraction is $\frac{3}{8}$
10 the fraction is $\frac{7}{8}$

Unit 6

1 $2\frac{1}{2}$ are shaded
2 $2\frac{3}{4}$ are shaded
3 $1\frac{3}{4}$ are shaded
4 $2\frac{4}{8}$ are shaded or $2\frac{1}{2}$ are shaded
5 $3\frac{1}{4}$ are shaded

ANSWERS

6

7

8

9

10

Unit 7

1 $\frac{3}{4}$
2 $\frac{7}{8}$
3 $\frac{1}{2}$
4 $\frac{3}{4}$
5 $\frac{3}{4}$
6 $\frac{1}{2}$
7 $\frac{1}{4}$
8 $\frac{5}{8}$

Unit 8

1
2
3
4
5

6 $\frac{1}{2}$ is equivalent to $\frac{2}{4}$ and $\frac{4}{8}$
7 $\frac{6}{8}$ is equivalent to $\frac{3}{4}$
8 $\frac{3}{4}$ is equivalent to $\frac{6}{8}$
9 $\frac{5}{4}$ is equivalent to $\frac{10}{8}$
10 $\frac{4}{2}$, $\frac{6}{3}$ and $\frac{8}{4}$

Unit 9

1 cup of flour
$\frac{1}{2}$ cup of sugar
$\frac{1}{2}$ teaspoon of salt
$\frac{1}{8}$ cup of cocoa
1 egg
40 chocolate chips
$\frac{1}{4}$ cup of milk
4 cups of flour
2 cups of sugar
2 teaspoons of salt
$\frac{1}{2}$ cup of cocoa
4 eggs
160 chocolate chips
1 cup of milk

Unit 10

1 $\frac{3}{4}$
2 $\frac{7}{8}$
3 20
4 9
5 24
6 $\frac{1}{4}$, 4
7 $\frac{1}{4}$
8 $\frac{3}{4}$ of a cup
9 9
10 $3

Unit 11

1 one third, $\frac{1}{3}$
2 one sixth, $\frac{1}{6}$
3 one fifth, $\frac{1}{5}$
4 one half, $\frac{1}{2}$
5 one tenth, $\frac{1}{10}$

6 fifth $\frac{1}{5}$

7 third $\frac{1}{3}$

8 sixth $\frac{1}{6}$ 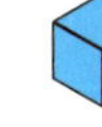

9 tenth $\frac{1}{10}$

10 two thirds $\frac{2}{3}$

Unit 12

1 – 4

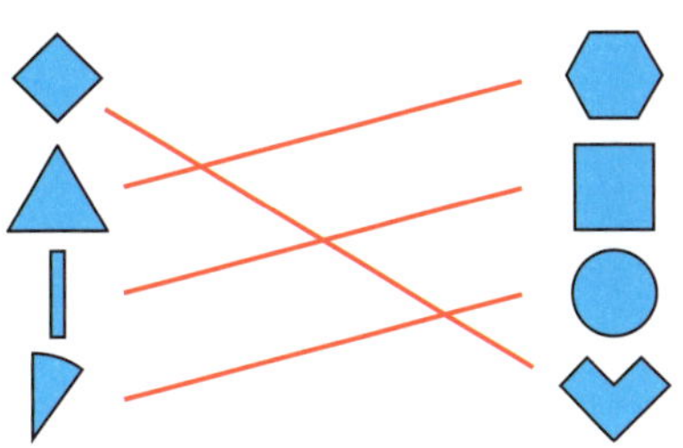

5 $\frac{1}{5}$
6 $\frac{1}{3}$
7 $\frac{1}{6}$
8 $\frac{1}{10}$
9 $\frac{1}{6}$
10 $\frac{1}{3}$

ANSWERS

Unit 13

1. ten thirds or $3\frac{1}{3}$
2. twelve fifths or $2\frac{2}{5}$
3. twelve tenths or $1\frac{2}{10}$
4. fifteen sixths or $2\frac{3}{6}$
5. fourteen sixths or $2\frac{2}{6}$
6.
7.
8.
9.
10.

Unit 14

1. $\frac{2}{3}$ of 6 equals 4
2. $\frac{2}{5}$ of 10 equals 4
3. $\frac{3}{10}$ of 10 equals 3
4. $\frac{4}{6}$ of 12 equals 8
5. $\frac{3}{8}$ of 16 equals 6
6. 8
7. 16
8. 10
9. 10
10. 20

Unit 15

1. $\frac{1}{5}$
2. $\frac{2}{5}$
3. $\frac{4}{10}$
4. $\frac{2}{5}$
5. $\frac{5}{8}$
6. $\frac{3}{8}$
7. $\frac{2}{5}$
8. $\frac{4}{5}$
9. $\frac{5}{6}$
10. $\frac{1}{3}$

Unit 16

1. $\frac{1}{2}$
2. $\frac{1}{2}$
3. $\frac{2}{5}$
4. $\frac{2}{3}$
5. $\frac{4}{10}$
6. $\frac{2}{6}$
7. $\frac{3}{8}$
8. $\frac{1}{10}$
9. $\frac{2}{5}$
10. $\frac{1}{4}$

Unit 17

1. more
2. same
3. more
4. more
5. more
6. $\frac{3}{8}$

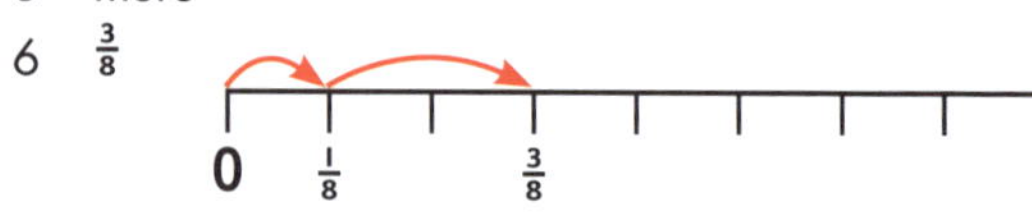

7. $\frac{3}{6}$ or $\frac{1}{2}$

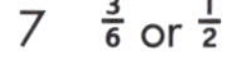

8. $\frac{5}{8}$

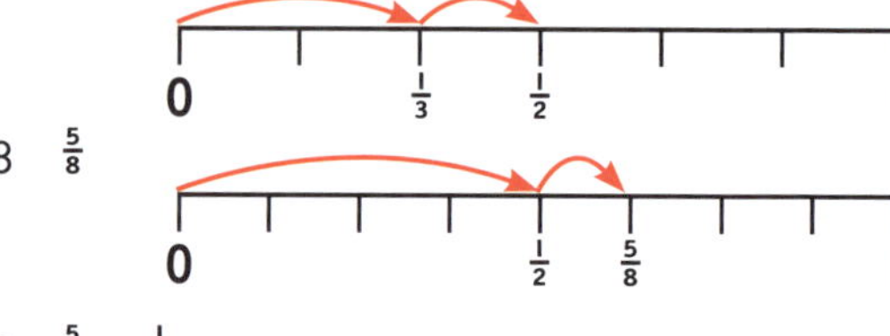

9. $\frac{5}{10}$ or $\frac{1}{2}$

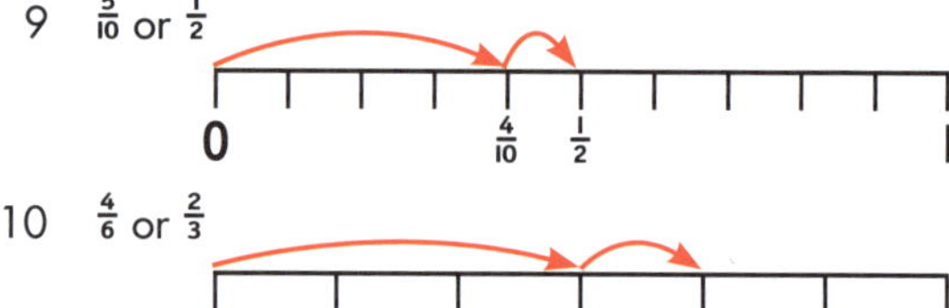

10. $\frac{4}{6}$ or $\frac{2}{3}$

0 $\frac{1}{2}$ $\frac{2}{3}$ 1

Unit 18

1. 1.3, $1\frac{3}{10}$
2. 2·6, $2\frac{3}{5}$
3. 1·5, $1\frac{1}{2}$
4. 0·6, $\frac{3}{5}$
5. 2·3, $2\frac{3}{10}$
6.
7. 
8. 
9.
10.

Unit 19

1. 1·25
2. 2·35
3. 2·14
4. 0·75
5. 3·3
6.
7. 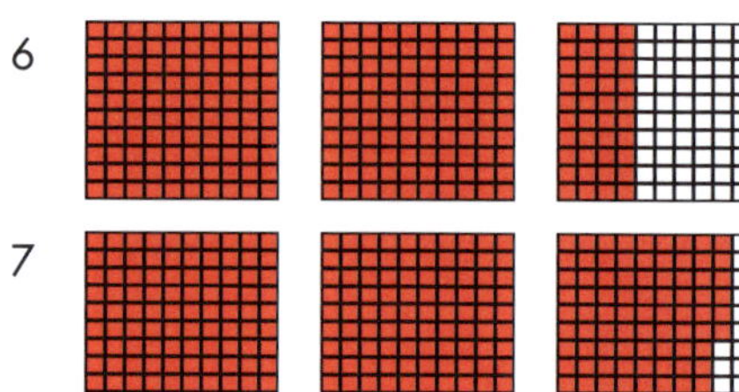

ANSWERS

8 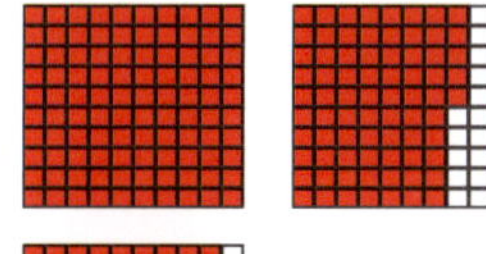

9 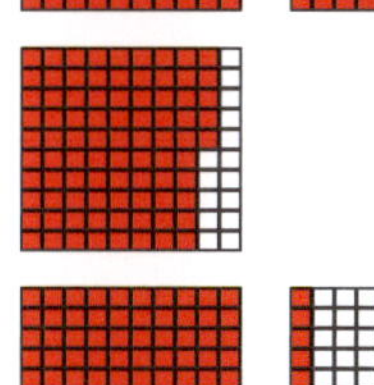

10 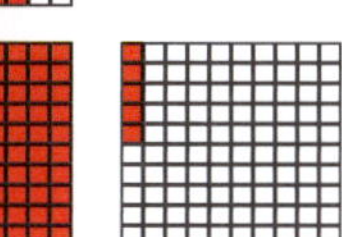

Unit 20

1 Neither; they are both $\frac{1}{8}$ away from 1
2 10
3 \$100
4 4
5 Max
6 100
7 Max
8 into quarters
9 $\frac{1}{8}$
10 $\frac{1}{2}$, 0·5, $\frac{50}{100}$

Test 1

1 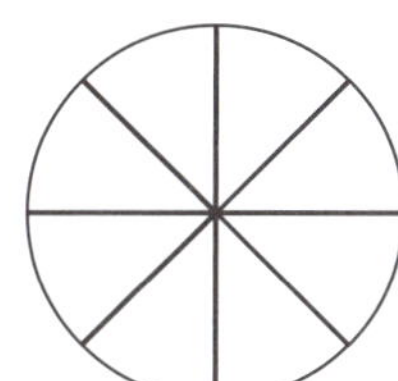

2 $\frac{1}{8}$
3 18
4  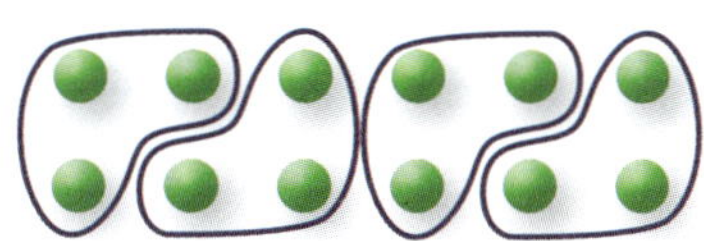

5 $\frac{1}{4}$
6 

0 1

7

0 1

8  

9 $\frac{3}{4}$ is larger
10 $\frac{3}{4}$

Test 2

1 one fifth, $\frac{1}{5}$
2 $\frac{1}{3}$
3 thirds, 8
4 

5

0 $\frac{3}{8}$ $\frac{3}{4}$ 1

6 $\frac{3}{8}$
7 more than
8 $\frac{1}{2}$
9 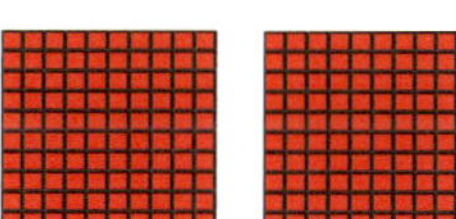

10 1·25

Back to Basics Fractions & Decimals Years 3–4

Copyright © 2012 Blake Education
Reprinted 2015, 2016, 2018

ISBN: 978 1 74215 932 4

Published by Pascal Press
PO Box 250
Glebe NSW 2037
www.pascalpress.com.au
contact@pascalpress.com.au

Author: Ann Baker
Publisher: Lynn Dickinson
Editor: Eliza Hope
Proofreader: Tim Learner
Design and illustration: Janice Bowles
Page layout and technical illustration: Louise Rhodes
Cover design: Deb Snibson, MAPG
Printed by Thumbprints

Reproduction and communication for educational purposes
The Australian Copyright Act 1968 (the Act) allows a maximum of one chapter or 10% of the pages of this work, whichever is the greater, to be reproduced and/or communicated by any educational institution for its educational purposes provided that the educational institution (or that body that administers it) has given a remuneration notice to the Copyright Agency Limited (CAL) under the Act.
For details of the CAL licence for educational institutions contact:
Copyright Agency Limited
Level 15, 233 Castlereagh Street
Sydney, NSW 2000

Reproduction and communication for other purposes
Except as permitted under the Act (for example a fair dealing for the purpose of study, research, criticism or review) no part of this book may be reproduced, stored in a retrieval system, communicated or transmitted in any form or by any means without prior written permission. All inquiries should be made to the publisher at the address above.
© Australian Curriculum, Assessment and Reporting Authority 2010.
This is a modified extract from the Australian Curriculum. ACARA neither endorses nor verifies the accuracy of the information provided and accepts no responsibility for incomplete or inaccurate information. You can find the unaltered and most up to date version of this material at http://www.australiancurriculum.edu.au/Home
This modified material is reproduced with the permission of ACARA.